Diaspora Missions Engagement in the Global North through Intercultural Campus Ministry: 'By and Beyond' Filipinos

Enoch Wan & Ria Martin

Diaspora Series of CDRR

Diaspora Missions Engagement in the Global North through Intercultural Campus Ministry: 'By and Beyond' Filipinos

Copyright 2023 © Western Academic Publishers

Enoch Wan & Ria Martin

Cover designed by Michael Maiocco

ISBN: 978-1-954692-20-6

CDRR (Center of Diaspora & Relational Research) @ https://www.westernseminary.edu/outreach/center-diaspora-relational-research

Western Academic Publishers

TABLE OF CONTENTS

LIST OF TABLES AND FIGURES

FIGURES

TABLES

FOREWORD

WHERE IS YOUR COMPANION?
A FORWORD BY MIRIAM ADENEY

"This is such a good party!" I said to a Filipino friend. But then I added, "Come to think of it, I have never been to a *bad* Filipino party."

There is a buzz that rises. Gentle quips ping-pong back and forth. Graceful hands proffer rice dishes. And noodles and pork and chicken. And coconut sweets and mangos and other fruits. Smiles shimmer. Songs break out. Floating in this warm sea, I feel buoyed up. Affection and delight lap around me. I feel cared for and secure. If, God forbid, there were a disaster, these people would flex, and those who have something to give would come forward to share with those in the group who need it.

Ria Llanto Martin is writing about this communal reality, where a person's sense of identity is rooted in treasured people rather than in his or her own individuality. She has focused particularly on the Filipino concept of *kapwa*. Centuries ago the European philosopher Rene Descartes defined his existence as an individual thinking being when he said, "I think, therefore I am." This became a foundation stone for Western philosophy. But some nonWestern people look at life differently. A friend from a more communal society tells me that he validates his existence because he sees himself as rooted in a specific group of people. He says, "I am related to these people, therefore I am." Not *Cogito, ergo sum,* in Descartes' words, but *Cognatus, ergo sum.* I am connected. It is in community that I see who I am.

When I lived in the Philippines, my neighbor's retired maid would sit on the low wall beside my path, swinging her rubber sandals. Wispy gray hair in a haphazard bun at the back of her head framed her saggy leathery skin, but her bright eyes sparkled. Whenever I emerged from my little house, she would call out, *"Saan ka pupunta?* Where are you going?"

"Diyan lang," I would respond with the stock answer. "Just over there." But she was not done. *"Nasaan ang kasama mo?* Where is your companion?"

In her view, a person should not go out anywhere alone. I should be accompanied. Who knew what might befall me? And naturally my destination was not my own private business, because, after all, I was part of a community.

This is the cultural context in which Ria Martin's insights have been seasoned. Today she directs a seminary intercultural program serving Middle Easterners, Indians, Africans, Latin Americans, and Anglo-Americans, as well as Filipinos. Previously Ria was a college professor, a life coach, and a campus outreach minister. To all these jobs she has brought relational skills which have been honed in her natal community.

vii

Ria is a hard worker. Campus outreach in the Philippines meant waiting daily in torrential heat for a crowded bus or jeep. Once she arrived on campus, Ria's witness might be rejected. Her disciples might relapse. Her trainees might get distracted. Still, she poured herself into the work with passion and diligence. Simultaneously, Ria studied for several graduate degrees, one after the other, culminating in a Ph.D. On the side she has continued to pick up technological skills and certifications so that she can be maximally useful. She is always pushing forward, growing and learning.

But not alone. She treasures her students and trainees and fellow workers. They are her dear companions. In particular, the Victory church, and its Every Nation congregation, have been like a family to Ria. They prepare their members for vigorous, informed global outreach. In all her ministry, Ria has been surrounded by their support.

Most of all, God has been her companion, as well as her core message. This is not just a vague God, a God of good ethics. No, this is a God who acts. This is the God who came close to us and took on human form, absorbed our curse and paid for it with blood, and then exploded back from death to generate power for new beginnings. Ria shares this good news with students. She also clings to it for her own personal hope and security and renewal. Beyond all other companions, God has chosen to be with her. Unthinkable, but true.

Loneliness is a huge problem in the world today. Sociological studies such as *Bowling Alone* by Robert Putnam document this. People like Ria who have been raised with the concept of *kapwa* may enrich the rest of us with this ethnotheological theme. And their parties may be foretastes of the greatest party of all, when the king of kings will be celebrated with dazzling jewels, light beyond electricity, billions of happy revelers, a river of life, and a tree with leaves for the healing of the nations.

Whether wiping drops of sweat from her forehead in the Philippines, or battling the rain of the Pacific Northwest, or unwinding to the languid work rhythms of the American South, Ria is never alone. Her life is studded with companions-- colleagues, clients, or simply fellow human beings. More important, God's presence is with her, whatever she is doing. She lives in the middle of community, rich in connections, both horizontal and vertical.

If my elderly neighbor Aling Barda were to call out to Ria, "Where is your companion?" Ria could answer, "Everywhere. My companions are everywhere."

ACKNOWLEGEMENT

This book is one of the many testaments of God's radical kindness in my life. He truly is about making impossible dreams possible.

To my mahal Forrest, who encouraged me to go back to school. Here is to a lifetime of continuously being transformed in Christ.

To my family in the Philippines, I miss you every day.

I am grateful for my time at Western Seminary and for my advisor and mentor, Dr. Enoch Wan. Thank you for pioneering for us diasporas in many trailblazing ways.

This book is dedicated to all the Filipinos scattered abroad. May you each find healing, refuge, and courage wherever you go. I pray that we will all find ourselves as an extension of God's peace and reconciliation of all nations.

To Pastor Steve Murrell and his family, thank you.

CHAPTER 1

INTRODUCTION

For Filipinos scattered across the globe, Jollibee is a home away from home. Jollibee is the number one fast-food chain in the Philippines, and it is known for its famous Chicken Joy (fried chicken) topped with gravy, sweet spaghetti, traditional *palabok* (noodle dish), and its famous *halo-halo* dessert. Jollibee embodies Filipino cultural values. It is a venue of choice for various celebrations such as baptisms, birthdays, and weddings that bring out the Filipino values of family, togetherness, and care. Jollibee is well visited internationally by Filipinos who now work or live abroad. They travel from miles away and wait in line for hours for a taste of home—truly a nostalgic experience. It has become a place of safety, familiarity, connection to kinsmen, and refuge for Filipinos living as foreigners

Background of Study

The Philippines is the thirteenth most populated country globally. With a total population of 109 million, approximately ten million Filipinos have scattered abroad; most reside in the United States.[1] More than eighty percent of the population has a religious affiliation of either Catholicism or Protestantism. With the population growth combined and their religious affiliation, Philip Jenkins, author of *The Next Christendom,* projected that the Philippines will be "home to the third or fourth-largest number of Christians on the planet by 2050."[2] In a similar vein, Jenkins quotes Kenyan scholar John Mbiti who observed that "the center of the church's universality, are no longer in Geneva, Rome, Athens, Paris, London, New York, but in Kinshasa, Buenos Aires, Addis Adaba and Manila."[3] Mark Noll shares the same observation on the unprecedented geographical redistribution in the Christian Church over the last fifty years, mostly due to evangelistic growth in Asia, Africa, Latin America, and the Islands of the South Pacific.[4] Furthermore, Afe Adogame refers to the steady increase of Christian migrants originating from the Majority World moving North as a "reverse mission"[5] that is irreversible in the future. From the

---

[1] "Philippines Population," accessed February 27, 2020, http://worldpopulationreview.com.

[2] Philip Jenkins, *The Next Christendom: The Coming of Global Christianity*, 3rd Ed. (Oxford ; New York: Oxford University Press, 2011), 1.

[3] Jenkins,1

[4] Mark A. Noll, *The New Shape of World Christianity: How American Experience Reflects Global Faith* (Downers Grove, IL: IVP Academic, 2009), 21.

[5] Afe Adogame, Raimundo Barreto, and Wanderley Pereira Da Rosa, eds., *Migration and Public Discourse in World Christianity* (Minneapolis: Fortress Press, 2019), 1.

"sixteenth century until the first half of the twentieth century, the Christians moved from North to South and from the West to the East. Since the second wave of the last century, World Christianity has become gradually polycentric."[6] By 2050, Jenkins added that Christianity would look different, changing from predominantly white into a blended culture of Asians, Africans, and Brazilians.

The Researcher

I was a campus missionary since 2006, serving college campuses in the Philippines before I moved to Seattle, WA, in 2012. I joined the staff of a local congregation in Seattle to pioneer their campus ministry. Even though Seattle is still considered one of the whitest cities in the United States, its demographics are shifting dramatically. "Foreign-born population grew 40% from 1990 to 2000,"[7] and the percentage of whites in Seattle dropped from 75.3% in the 1990s to 64.5% in 2018.[8] The city's most diverse neighborhoods are in South Seattle, where most immigrants have initially moved and stayed. One will notice an array of Asian cuisines in the university area, a few up North and the majority in Downtown and South Seattle. Like the city, many churches in Seattle display diversity, some are predominantly white, with a handful of multiethnic churches.

My ministry transition from the Philippines to the United States exposed unfamiliar missiological paradigms. Once, a potential financial partner said to me, "Why are you coming to the United States to become a campus missionary here? We usually send missionaries to your country." Some Filipinos from the Seattle congregation expressed excitement about starting an all-Filipino service separate from the multiethnic worship gathering on Sundays. A Filipino friend suggested I go to poverty-stricken nations in Asia or Africa, where "the *real* mission takes place." At first, an option to target a more focused ministry for international students was ideal; as an international myself, my situation would be most relatable, making me an effective minister. My experiences as a Filipino campus missionary to Seattle, WA, introduced new perspectives on mission and how one decides to participate in it. It became self-evident that missions is driven by how one understands the mission.

For much of my stay in Seattle as a missionary, I found myself retreating to Jollibee, my ethnic enclave. It felt safe, familiar, and reminiscent of home. Nevertheless, as a missionary in a diverse city, I wondered if having a target people group would be necessary.

After five years of pioneering a campus ministry in Seattle, the ministry became home to both locals and international students. Two campus leaders in

---

[6] Klaus Koscherke and Adrian Hermann, "Polycentric Structures in the History of World Christianity" (Wiesbaden: Harrassowitz, 2014) PDF.

[7] "Seattle, United States Population (2021) - Population Stat," World Statistical Data, accessed October 27, 2021, https://populationstat.com/united-states/seattle.

[8] Rico Quirindongo, "About Seattle - OPCD | Seattle.Gov," accessed October 27, 2021, http://www.seattle.gov/opcd/population-and-demographics/about-seattle#raceethnicity.

the area visited our campus ministry hoping to find some answers to their question, "How did you get your ministry to be so diverse?" A Filipino pastor back home asked if the campus ministry was mainly Filipino, somewhat surprised and excited that it was indeed a representation of locals and internationals. Many locals, as well as other nations, were represented in the campus ministry. Some international students were from Ghana, China, Myanmar, Nepal, Vietnam, Dominican Republic, Japan, Eritrea, Malawi, South Korea, and Indonesia. We birthed a campus ministry where the international and local students integrate into one local—and intercultural—campus ministry. My personal story is what Bob Roberts describes as "glocal," which is "the seamless integration between the local and global"[9] A short description of his book on *Glocalization* said:

"... if you want to know where and how the church is going to grow, think local and global. That connection is affecting the church in ways that never could have been imagined ... And it is creating unprecedented opportunities for individuals and churches- for you and your church- to live out their faith."[10]

The Purpose of this Book:

This book aims to present an understanding and relational ways to engage first-generation Filipino missionaries in diaspora missions through an intercultural campus ministry.

Below is background information that can be helpful to readers of this book:

- For first-generation Filipino missionaries, their monocultural background impedes their diaspora missions engagement in various cities in the global north. Diaspora missions engagement surfaced new queries regarding our participation in missions. Should missionaries from the majority world participate in the global north? If so, what is Good News for the wealthy nations? What if the host city perceives missionaries from the majority world negatively? Should Filipinos limit their participation in missions reaching only their people group?
- Bryan Loritts, president and founder of *Kainos* Movement[11] said, "we have an unprecedented opportunity where the church is forced to get back to her first-century roots, to go back to the days when Jews and Gentiles were doing life together, loving one another, all in the context of the local church."[12] The church of Jesus Christ should model integration by breaking down barriers such as gender, ethnicity, and

---

[9] Robert, Bob Jr., *Glocalization: How Followers of Jesus Engage a Flat World*, (Grand Rapids,MI:Zondervan, 2007), 14.

[10] Robert, Bob Jr., *Glocalization: How Followers of Jesus Engage a Flat World*, (Grand Rapids,MI:Zondervan, 2007).

[11] *Kainos* Movement is an organization founded by Pastor Bryan Loritts, committed to seeing multicultural churches in America, 80/20 rule, become the new normal.

[12] Bryan Loritts, *Right Color, Wrong Culture: The Type of Leader Your Organization Needs to Become Multiethnic*, New Edition. (Chicago: Moody Publishers, 2014), 103.

economic diversity of the status quo. The projected trajectory of geographical redistribution and reverse mission should alert pastors and church planters that despite this phenomenon, 97.5 percent of US churches (for instance) remain homogenous to this day.[13]

- The aftermath of multicultural churches today is that there are no people of color among white churches. The following reflective question is for the Majority World missionary to the US: would I reverse that concern of no white people among colored churches?

The Readership of this Book:

a.) First-generation Filipino (or from the Majority World) missionaries and church planters who are ready to move their church from monocultural practices to becoming an intercultural church.

b.) Christians and leaders who want to be involved in intercultural campus ministry in the global north.

c.) Christian leaders (i.e., pastors and missions executives, etc.,) and trainers (i.e., faculty members of seminary and Bible school) who are interested in knowing the challenges of first-generation diaspora missionaries serving in the post-Christendom West.

Definition of Key Terms

Campus Ministry – a Christian ministry to college students in universities or community colleges.

Diaspora Missiology – a contemporary missions paradigm to participate in the current global shift of Christianity. Diaspora missions focus on ministering to and through diasporas.[14] A whole section on diaspora missions is in chapter two, the review of related literature.

Global North – the developed, wealthy nations from North America, Europe, Asia, and Oceania. They are often known as the West or First World.[15] It is a socio-economic status rather than a geographical identity. Countries like Australia and New Zealand are part of the global north even though they are geographically within the southern hemisphere.

Global South – a political term coined by Carl Oglesby in the 1950s about the global northern and southern divide and US dominance over the South. This divide emphasizes a country's economic conditions, an imaginary demarcation line between wealthy nations and developing nations.[16] "Majority world" is the

---

[13] Loritts, 102.

[14] Enoch Wan, *Diaspora Missiology: Theory, Methodology, and Practice*, (Portland, OR: Institute of Diaspora Studies, 2011), 131.

[15] Mark Owuor Otieno, "What is Global South?" accessed October 8, 2020, https:www.worldatlas.com.

[16] Otieno, "What is Global South?" accessed October 8, 2020, https://www.worldatlas.com.

preferred term the author will use throughout this paper, a non-derogatory term emphasizing the population rather than the nation's economic condition.

Glocalization – "is another term for the flat earth that describes the seamless integration between the local and global."[17]

Intercultural Campus Ministry (ICM) – integrating local and international students into one local campus ministry. A section in this book explains why the researcher prefers intercultural rather than the more famous multicultural.

International Student Ministry (ISM) – a campus ministry targeting international students, whether graduates or undergraduates, by a local church or campus ministry organization. Hospitality is one of the missional practices of this ministry.

Mission – a process by which Christians (individuals) and the Church (institutional) continue on and carry out the *missio Dei* of the Triune God ("mission") at both individual and institutional levels spiritually (saving souls) and socially (ushering in *shalom*) for redemption, reconciliation, and transformation ("missions").[18]

Missions – ways and means of accomplishing "the mission" which has been entrusted by the Triune God to the Church and Christians.[19]

Participatory Action Research – a method of research inquiry to improve an organization or a setting, designed and conducted mostly by practitioners who analyze the data to improve their practice.[20]

Relational Realism Paradigm – a "conceptual framework for understanding reality based on the interactive connections between personal beings/Beings."[21]

The Organization of the Book

There are six chapters in this book, with "introduction" at the beginning and "conclusion" at the end. Chapter 2 provides readers the background of the book and Chapter 3 introduces the participants of the research. Chapter 4 covers the topic of diaspora missions through intercultural campus ministry and Chapter 5 derives missiological implications from the research findings.

For the sake of smooth reading and simple reference, "I" is used to designate Ria Martin who conducted the research for her dissertation and shares her findings with our readers.

---

[17] Robert, Bob Jr., *Glocalization*, 14.

[18] Enoch Wan, *Diaspora Missions to International Students* (Portland, OR:Western Seminary Press, 2019), 10.

[19] Wan, *Diaspora Missions to International Students,*10.

[20] Leo Rigsby, PowerPoint Presentation, IET, George Madison University

[21] Enoch Wan and Mark Hedinger, *Relational Missionary Training: Theology, Theory & Practice* (Skyforest, CA: Urban Loft Publishers, 2017), 14.

CHAPTER 2

BACKGROUND KNOWLEDGE OF THIS BOOK

Introduction

When I moved to Seattle, WA, to pioneer a campus ministry, I met an international student from China named "Kay."[22] She had just moved to Seattle a couple of months beforehand to begin her studies at a community college. Kay believed that by avoiding her Chinese community in the school and hanging out with locals and other internationals would force her to learn English efficiently. I offered help by teaching her to read English using the New Living Translation Bible. Eventually, she started coming to our church, became a Christian, and on her baptism day, gave up the Buddha necklace she had been wearing since she was a child. In April 2018, I flew to Los Angeles to attend her graduation at the University of California, Los Angeles (UCLA). She stopped by Seattle to visit me before she traveled back to China. Our friendship continues to thrive, even though we are thousands of miles away from each other.

This story is an illustration of two diasporas who voluntarily moved to the United States for different reasons. A Filipino missionary called by God to pioneer a campus ministry and an international student for academic pursuit. This type of engagement in missions is known as the diaspora missions movement.

Diaspora Missions

One often associates the term diaspora with the dispersion of the Jews from their homelands, but this is just one (biblical) instance of such a phenomenon. A diaspora may be a forced or voluntary movement. Dispersion with the intention to expand economic or political gain is voluntary diaspora. Forced migration refers to persecution or exile. Sam George, an expert on global migration and diaspora mission, defines diaspora as sowing, scattering, or dispersion.[23] Although some scholars argue for the exclusive use of diaspora to Jewish dispersion, George and the contributors of *Diaspora Christianities: Global Scattering and Gathering of South Asian Christians* dedicated this book to the Christian faith of the dispersed people from Southern Asia. Afe Adogame, a leading scholar on African diasporas, refers to it as "people of faith on the move."[24] His book, *Migration and Public Discourse in World Christianity*, focuses on people of faith on the move, displaced people who carry their faith wherever

---

[22] Pseudonym.

[23] Sam George, Diaspora Christianities: *Global Scattering And Gathering Of South Asian Christians* (Fortress Press, 2019), 4.

[24] Adogame, et al, 2.

they go. In return, it contributes to their resilience as they manage the tension of living in a foreign land without breaking their connection with their homeland. Enoch Wan, a pioneer in the field who has published more than fifteen books on diaspora mission, is himself part of the global Chinese diaspora. Wan's study on the concept of dispersion or scattering in the Old Testament encompasses seven root words expressed differently. For instance, the word *napas,* which only occurred three times in the OT, means "the idea of scattering involves the act of the shattering." While *pazar* means "to scatter abroad freely."[25] In the New Testament, two Greek words emanate, scattered (*diaspora*) and to scatter (*diaspeiro*).[26] He summarizes his points that dispersions or scattering are realities found in the Bible. God is in full control, both in the dispersion as well as the regathering. Based on Jenkins' projections on the shift of Christianity, as a missiologist, Wan believes that diaspora missiology is the appropriate missiological response to the new reality of the twenty-first century.[27]

Diaspora missions, as Wan defines it, is:

Christians' participation in God's redemptive missions to evangelize their kinsmen on the move, and through them to reach out to natives in their homelands and beyond. There are four types of diaspora missions, *to, through, by and beyond, and with.*[28]

William Murrell illustrates these four types of diaspora in a case study on Every Nation Ministries, entitled, "From Every Campus to Every Nation." Murrell wrote, "even though American missionaries planted the church in Manila, it does not promote 'West to the rest' mentality or the traditional mission' paradigm."[29] Murrell narrated stories of the diasporic missions' movement within Every Nation. Examples are stories of an Iranian convert married to a Filipina who attended a Filipino diaspora church in Dubai (diaspora missions *to*). Currently based in the United States—this Iranian convert is reaching out to his kinsmen, Iranian Muslims in the United States (diaspora missions *through*). Victory Los Baños, Philippines, has a thriving international student ministry. The university's International Rice Research Institute program drew students from Bhutan, Cambodia, China, India, Nigeria, and Nepal (diaspora missions *by and beyond*). One Filipino missionary eventually served Nepal, reconnected with those who were part of the

---

[25] The seven root words of how diaspora is used in the Old Testament are 1) *gola* (exiles)/*gala* (remove)/*galut* (captivity, 2) *zara* (spread, winnow), 3) *nadah* (banish), 4) *napas* (scatter), 5) *pus* (disperse), 6) *pazar* (scatter abroad), and 7) *parad* (separate). See *Diaspora Missiology: Theory, Methodology, and Practice,* 36-44 for details of these biblical terms.

[26] Wan, *Diaspora Missiology,* 44–52.

[27] Wan, *Diaspora Missiology,* 5.

[28] For detailed description of diaspora missions see Wan, *Diaspora Missiology,* 6.

[29] William Murrell, Chapter Ten, "From Every Campus to Every Nation: Case Studies of Diaspora Mission" in Enoch Wan et al., *Diaspora Missions to International Students* (Portland, OR: Western Seminary Press, 2019), 173-183.

international student ministry in Los Baños then, and helped establish a local Every Nation congregation in Nepal (diaspora missions *with*). Over the last twenty-five years, Every Nation has grown to over 400 churches in over eighty nations, a product of a multi-directional and polycentric missions' movement with its most extraordinary missionary dynamism from one particular church in Manila, Victory Church, Murrell concluded.[30]

Filipino Diasporas

The statistical records on global migration are analogous with current projections on Filipinos becoming the fourth largest Christian community on the planet.[31] Globally, migration reached an all-time high of 272 million international migrants worldwide, comprising twenty-six million refugees, 3.5 million asylum seekers, and over forty-one million displaced internationally.[32] Regionally, Europe hosts the most massive immigrant population worldwide. At the country level, the United States hosts fifty-one million migrants out of the 272 million international migrants worldwide, as claimed by the United Nations Department of Economic and Social Affairs and *ined* (*Institut National d 'etudes Demographiques*).

In the late twentieth century, Filipinos were among the fastest-growing populations of immigrants in the United States. By the early twenty-first century, they constituted the third-largest Asian population in the United States after the Chinese and Indians.[33] Today, Filipino immigrants represent the fourth largest origin group, after Mexico, India, and China. Most Filipino immigrants reside in the United States; other top destinations are Saudi Arabia, Canada, Japan, United Arab Emirates, and Australia.[34]

Luis Pantoja, Sadiri Tira, and Wan published *Scattered: The Filipino Global Presence* to document this massive migration. In the 1970s, Filipinos experienced a forced massive dispersion mainly due to their country's unfortunate political and economic condition. Filipino families sought opportunities abroad by working as seafarers, nannies, nurses, and engineers. They are called the Overseas Filipino Workers (OFWs). The forced migration presented opportunities to contribute to the crippling economy and, consequently, propagated their faith in their workplace. Filipino diasporas' adaptability enabled them to contextualize churches creatively in buses, ocean liners, and hospitals. Filipino Missiologists and mission agencies discerned this opportunity. Partnership with the Philippine government established

[30] Murrell, *Diaspora Missions to International Students*, 175

[31] Jenkins, 1.

[32] "The Number of International Migrants Reaches 272 Million, Continuing an Upward Trend in all World Regions, Says UN," United Nations, accessed February 26, 2020, https://www.un.org.

[33] Luis Hassan Gallardo and Jeanne Batalova, "Filipino Immigrants in the United States," Migration Policy Institute, accessed March 9, 2020, https://immigrationtounitedstates.org.

[34] Gallardo and Batalova, "Filipino Immigrants in the United States," accessed March 9, 2020, https://immigrationtounitedstates.org.

equipping seminars, customizing OFWs 'training involving evangelism and discipleship.'

In a case study by Tira and Stuart Lightbody, the First Filipino Alliance Church (FFAC)[35] in Edmonton, Alberta, started as a small Bible study group for Filipino university students that grew to become a home base center for Filipino International Network (FIN).[36] Its humble beginnings happened in the living room of a student's housing complex, where regular meetings and Bible study groups take place. This Filipino Bible study group gave birth to a church that serves Filipinos (Filipino Alliance Church) and continued to serve other diaspora groups, illustrating FIN's cyclical and glocal nature. Its mandate to reach Filipinos for Christ extended beyond Canada and successfully sent missionaries to other nations.[37]

Filipino churches have been participating in diaspora missions, whether in Dubai or Canada. Philippines Missions Association (PMA), for instance, has been instrumental in "mobilizing, coordinating and supporting over 3,300 cross-cultural workers as well as training and enabling more than 500,000 Filipino evangelicals employed overseas to see themselves as Kingdom ambassadors."[38]

Tira's ethnographic research on *Filipino Kingdom Workers* provides testimonials of Filipino diasporas, the Overseas Filipino Workers (OFWs), taking the gospel to other nations, such as Europe and Hongkong. He claimed that this strategy is the most cost-effective mission strategy; for decades before, only very wealthy nations had the resources to send.

These research studies and statistics are pieces of evidence that Filipino diasporas thrive in other nations, professionally and missionally, establishing Christian faith from the time of Spanish colonization. Their exposure to hardships and natural disasters developed their adaptability, resilience, and creativity when faced with opposition and challenges, making them successful as ministers of the gospel, especially in creative access nations.

Anthropologists have noted that "Filipino culture and language can be described as a fusion of basic Malay traits with foreign influences. Consequently, people in the Philippines are racially and culturally heterogeneous. The Filipinos in foreign places are "natural witnesses of Jesus

---

[35] First Filipino Alliance Church first started as a bible study group of five Filipino university students in Edmonton, Canada. It grew to multiple Filipino congregations. In 2017, they changed their name to Central Edmonton Alliance Church to support the vision of the alliance of reaching all peoples for God's kingdom. Accessed December 7, 2020, http://www.ceachurch.ca/church-history.

[36] Filipino International Network Is "A Catalytic Movement Of Christians Committed to Motivate and Mobilize Filipinos Globally to Partner for Worldwide Missions." Accessed December 7, 2020, Https://Www.Ceachurch.Ca/Church-History.

[37] Sadiri Joy Tira And Stuart Lightbody, "A Cyclical, Glocal Diaspora Congregation: A Case Study of the First Filipino Alliance Church," 1984, PDF.

[38] "Country: Philippines," Lausanne Movement, accessed October 22, 2020, https://www.lausanne.org/tbd/country-profiles/philippines).

Christ with great potential for impact wherever they are due to the following factors: religiously being Catholic, linguistically being English speaking, socially being friendly, pleasant and adaptable."[39]

Viernes and De Guzman wrote an article on "Filipino Teachers' Experiences of Supportive Relationships with Colleagues: A Narrative-biographical Inquiry," which disclosed significant themes that describe "how Filipino teachers as relational people experience and interpret supportive relationships in the school setting."[40] Supportive relationships were interpreted as a life-giving force, an extension of one's family, a reciprocal process, and a work still in progress.

Bainer and Didham (1994) in a study entitled, "Mentoring and Other Support Behaviors in Elementary Schools" posit that supportive relationships in the workplace have always been a significant concern for workers. The same study revealed the results of a Gallup poll conducted on 1,200 workers who ranked supportive relationships as among the ten strongest motivational factors, higher than money and status. [41]

Viernes and de Guzman quote Keltchtermans point that good working conditions are necessary to achieve maximum performance of professional tasks, particularly relationships with colleagues:

The Filipino teacher is a classic example of relational genius. Through his constant dealings and encounters with administrators, colleagues, students, and the community, he gets to understand his *being and existence* (emphasis mine) in a school setting.[42]

Even though Filipinos are highly relational, they are also aware of the tension and conflicts in the workplace and accept them as part of their daily lives. Because they see their workplace as a community, an extension of the family, enduring the difficulties in teaching is made easy knowing that help is expected from the school community. They state:

This idea of a conducive atmosphere is aptly described as *knowledge communities* (emphasis mine) by Olson and Craig (2001), where relationships among teachers become the expression and enactment of their personal practical knowledge that develops as they learn to reconstruct

[39] Enoch Wan and Sadiri Joy Tira, "The Filipino Experience in Diaspora Missions: A Case Study of Mission Initiatives from the Majority World Churches," PDF, 32.

[40] Sr. Ramona M. Viernes, O.P. and Allan B. de Guzman, "Filipino Teachers' Exeprinces of Supportive Relationships with Colleagues: A Narrative-biographical Inquiry," Asia Pacific Education Review2005, Vol. 6, No. 2, 137-142. By Education Research Institute.

[41] Viernes and de Guzman, "Filipino Teachers' Experiences of Supportive Relationships with Colleagues."

[42] Viernes and de Guzman, "Filipino Teachers' Experiences of Supportive Relationships with Colleagues."

meaning in their interactions with one another (Ayers, 1980; Casey, 1993; Paley, 1979).[43]

I also quote Felipe De Leon, a Filipino professor of Art Studies:

Filipinos at their best are highly nurturing, caring, sharing people with a strong maternal orientation and definitely not loners. Filipinos, because of their genius in interpersonal communication and a nurturing, caring attitude, excel in the service professions or industry. They are the most highly relational people in the world.[44]

Filipinos like to do things together and are hardly alone. Community is one of the key points in understanding the Filipino worldview, Jocano claims.[45] They will bring others when they travel, eat, pray, or celebrate. They appreciate activities that will bring people together. They view the world as a whole, an Eastern thinking common among Asians. This orientation focuses on "harmony, holism and the mutual influence of everything on almost everything else."[46] Kaiping Peng identified three principles that govern Eastern thinking, the principle of Change, the principle of Contradiction, and the principle of Relationship, or Holism.[47] For Filipinos and cultures with Eastern thinking, they believe nothing exists in isolation and everything is connected. They search for relationships between things. The desire to keep or pursue harmony or find the Middle Way is apparent in negotiations and decision-making:

Thinking in terms or 'both/and' rather than 'either/or' also applies to negotiation. Someone who thinks from a 'Western' perspective will tend to choose between two clear-cut alternatives, either option A or B. 'Eastern' negotiation implies thinking in terms of 'both/and,' and thus means exploring whether option A and B can be combined.[48]

Despite these positive traits, OFWs continue to experience marginalization in their contexts. Athena Gorospe tackles marginalization experienced by Filipinos in two ways: socially and structurally invisible and subaltern experiences.[49] Most OFWs have college degrees,[50] yet they come to another

---

[43] Viernes and de Guzman, "Filipino Teachers' Experiences of Supportive Relationships with Colleagues."

[44] "What makes Filipino, Filipino?" Embassy of the Philippines, accessed November 4, 2021, https://athenspe.dfa.gov.ph/newsroom/community-news.

[45] Felipe Landa Jacano is a distinguished Filipino anthropologist, a quote from his book *Filipino World: Ethnographic of Local Knowledge.*

[46] Edwin Hoffman And Arjan Verdooren, *Diversity Competence: Cultures Don't Meet, People Do* (Boston, Ma: Cabi, 2019), 202.

[47] Edwin Hoffman And Arjan Verdooren, 203.

[48] Edwin Hoffman And Arjan Verdooren, 206.

[49] Athena Gorospe, "Case Study: Overseas Filipino Workers" LOP 62 G, Lausanne Movement, accessed January 1, 2020, https://www.lausanne.org.

[50] Before Filipinos migrated to other countries as OFW or agriculturalist, wealthy families, *mestizas and mestizos,* sent their children abroad for education. Philippines' national hero, Dr.

country to serve as a nanny, cook, or seafarer. For instance, a Filipino doctor can often only serve as a nurse in another country or a Filipino dentist as a dental technician. In other words, they will always be only second in command—a subaltern.[51]

Remigio Jr. quotes Scoenberger's article in the Los Angeles Times (Scoenberger 1994) describing overseas Filipino workers as:

> Distinctive among the huddled masses of global economic migrants, overseas Filipinos represent the elite, high end of the labor market. They are generally well-educated and usually accomplished speakers of English. Nevertheless, like other itinerant workers, they lack opportunities in the dysfunctional Philippine economy. So women with college degrees serve as maids in Tokyo and Hongkong. Semi-skilled laborers toil in Kuwait while Filipino seamen ply the oceans on the world's ships. Filipino business graduates dominate the mid-level management ranks of many multinational corporations in Southeast Asia, earning wages they couldn't dream of at home.[52]

In 2010, 48.1% of maids in Hong Kong were Filipinos. They had college degrees in nursing and were hired as domestic helpers or maids, which stereotyped Filipinas as domestic helpers worldwide. In other words, when Filipinas travel, they are immediately perceived as domestic helpers. Leonora Torres is one of the 290,600 foreign maids working in Hong Kong. Like most of them, she is on call day and night. She is paid $650 a month to be available 24 hours a day, six days a week, which is a quarter of the cost of such help in France.[53] Her employer justifies that $650 is a good salary for Hong Kong, which is $144 more than the minimum wage for local maids. Lenora has a diploma in telegram transcription. She left her family to work in Hong Kong in order to send her children to school. This is a common story among OFWs, leaving the family to send some monetary help. However, according to the Hong Kong Labor

---

Jose Rizal, is a testament to that. Education is one of the values of Filipinos. Families from the provinces send their children to universities in Manila, with most of their resources, sometimes with live chicken and vegetables, knowing that education will provide a way out of poverty for Filipino poor families. This value continues to make Filipinos in the United States, ages 25 and older, have a much higher education rate compared to both the native- and overall foreign-born populations. Almost half of Filipino immigrants (49 percent) reported having at least a bachelor's degree in 2018, compared to 33 percent of the U.S. born and 32 percent of all immigrant adults. Gallardo and Batalova, "Filipino Immigrants in the United States," accessed October 22, 2020, https://www.migrationpolicy.org.

[51] The term Subaltern can be traced back to its post-colonial roots and critical theory, popularized by an Italian Marxist, Antonio Gramsci. It is associated with the lower social class, the Other group, the marginalized in the society ruled over by an elitist group. Vinayak Chaturvedi, "A Critical Theory of Subalternity: Rethinking Class in Indian Historiography," https://lh.journals.yorku.ca/index.php/lh/article/view/15042 (November 25, 2020).

[52] Luis L. Pantoja Jr, Sadiri Joy B. Tira, and Enoch Wan, eds., *Scattered: The Filipino Global Presence*, 1st edition. (Manila, Philippines: LifeChange Publishing, 2004), 10.

[53] Julien Brygo, "Filipino Maids for Export," *Le Monde Diplomatique*, last modified October 1, 2011, accessed October 16, 2021, https://mondediplo.com/2011/10/12maids.

Department, 10% of domestic workers complain against their employers every year for non-payment of wages, infringement of contracts, ill-treatment, or sexual harassment. Lenora was beaten, insulted, and mistreated while lending her services to a foreign land. Some of the stories of maids across the globe are horrific and unimaginable.

While Scoenberger description of OFWs as "elite, high end of labor market," San Juan Jr. describes a section in his book, *From Exile to Diaspora*, "Our resources are our bodies," as cheap labor to the world:

> We still find evidence of the routine attitude of Euro-Americans to Filipinos as good only as the manual work in the fields—those images of Filipino workers in California and Hawaii plantations still predominate in the consciousness of the EuroAmerican majority. In the past, Filipinos were considered petty merchandise listed next to 'fertilizer' or 'manure' by farm proprietors. Today the demand for OFW promoted by presidents "our improvement in our international status as a supplier of cheap labor and other resources to the industrialized metropoles- a comparative advantage to our lasting disadvantage.[54]

Gorospe states:

> ...the pain of marginality is made acute by being regarded as mere instruments of policy and by being subjected to ethnic, economic, and social differentiation. Migrant workers are often seen as mere objects to advance the interests of both the country of destination and the country of origin, without regard to the personal and family fragmentation and disempowerment that this produces.[55]

In Gorospe's case study, she acknowledged a restraining force known as the concept of Otherness.[56] In chapter three, I expound on the concept of Otherness and proposed *Kapwa*, as a redemptive analogy, a Filipino Scriptural response to marginalization.

Intercultural Campus Ministry

When I moved to Seattle from the Philippines to pioneer a campus ministry, I was given the option to start with either international students or locals. Starting with international students would seem a good fit for an international

---

[54] E. San Juan Jr, *From Exile To Diaspora: Versions Of The Filipino Experience In The United States*, 1st edition. (Routledge, 2000), 1.

[55] Gorospe, "Case Study: Overseas Filipino Workers" LOP 62 G, accessed January 1, 2020, https://www.lausanne.org.

[56] Otherness "which is positive and accepting can help embrace diversity, while negative and discriminating Otherness entails unhealthy judgements." Paul Woods, in "God, Israel, the Church and the Other: Otherness as a Theological Motif in Diaspora Mission" in Sadiri Joy Tira and Tetsunao Yamamori, *Scattered and Gathered: A Global Compendium of Diaspora Missiology* (Eugene, OR: Wipf and Stock Publisher, 2016), 134-145. A section in the final dissertation will explore this further.

minister like me who recently moved to a new city. It would have been easy to find connection points (living as a foreigner) and potentially minimize barriers in cross-cultural missions. For some reason having an area of focus did not seem to be a priority, or maybe my lack of cross-cultural training pushed me to think, "Well, let us see whom God will bring into our campus ministry." During the first few months of ministry, we had four local students. I met an international student from a local dance studio, and we started spending time together. Bringing her to our small gathering then did not seem to bother her. Learning English was her priority, and the locals seemed very excited to learn from another culture as well. She would come over and bring tasty dishes popular in her country. She started bringing in her classmates, international students from China, South Korea, Taiwan, and Japan. Our international students from different parts of Asia were compelled to speak English rather than their mother tongue. It is advantageous for the group, leaving no one behind in the conversation. As simple as playing board games and sharing meals became our weekly Friday night occasion. Once, we accidentally hosted an International Thanksgiving. Our international students brought dishes to share. We had California maki, Asian noodles, *adobo,* along with Turkey, green beans, and mashed potatoes. We continue to find our campus ministry becoming a home for both international and local students. For the past eight years of serving as a campus missionary in Seattle, I realized that we were simply faithful to the students God led into our ministry, whether they were locals or international students. I did not create a separate strategy for each one based on their ethnicity. We combined social events, attended one Bible study group using the same story format material, and joined worship gatherings for locals and international students. It was a seamless integration between local and global or international students. So in hindsight, I call it an intercultural campus ministry. Intercultural Campus Ministry is an integration of local and international students into one local campus chapter. After deep reflection and research, ICM succinctly is a convergence of campus ministries and international student ministries. The following section will explain why.

Campus Ministries and Their Impact Beyond University Walls

Many campus ministries view universities as a harvest field and a very strategic one. The following section reveals contemporary campus ministries' involvement in missions and church planting. The first two campus ministries, Campus Crusade for Christ and Intervarsity Christian Fellowship, are purely campus organizations. The last two, Student Church Planting Experience and Every Nation Ministries, are hybrids of campus ministry and church planting.

Campus Crusade for Christ

Bill Bright and other young men formed the Fellowship of a Burning Heart, a movement devoted to evangelizing the world's youth for Christ. This fellowship devoted themselves to an hour each day for Scripture and prayer, called for a life of devotion, purity, and chastity, and formed small groups that would multiply evangelistically. Bright emphasized the importance of academic preparation, but the first and primary task is to be missionaries to the world. He rounded up a dozen of his classmates to distribute "gospel bombs" on the campuses. He valued not just the salvation of individual souls but for the redemption of the whole nation.

During his days in Princeton, he recruited his college students to distribute gospel bombs throughout the university, which disturbed the security of the campus but did not quench Bright's fervor for evangelism. The Fellowship of a Burning Heart[57] was a movement devoted to evangelizing the youth of the world for Christ.[58] This fellowship devoted themselves to an hour each day for Scripture and prayer, called for a life of devotion, purity, and chastity, formed small groups that would multiply itself evangelistically, hosted "College Briefing Conferences" where they invited other colleges from around the country. In these College Briefing Conferences, students received their "marching orders" annually before heading to the "battle." They used military verbiage to promote evangelism on their campuses, especially in response to the perceived threat of communism in America. College meetings played a significant role in American evangelicalism, particularly in foreign missions. CRU (at that time, Campus Crusade for Christ) used tools such as the Four Spiritual Laws and the *Jesus Film* to remote overseas villages, conducted ministries in cafeterias, dormitories, fraternity, and sorority meetings, locker rooms, and tapped Greek life and college sports. Turner argues that,

> The adaptability and marketing prowess of parachurch organizations like CRU is not the only reason for the post-1945 vitality of American evangelicalism; basic evangelical message appeals to America, cultural adaptation and aggressive salesmanship.[59]

Explo'72 is a weeklong festival known as the religious Woodstock, where 85,000 college and high school students converged for a rock music festival. Explo'72 was the book's cover photo for *Bill Bright and the Campus Crusade for Christ: The Renewal of Evangelicalism in Postwar of America*. The emotions depicted in the picture showed devotion to God and the abandonment of the cares of the world. "What began with college students has since grown into the largest international Christian ministry in the world, reaching beyond students

---

[57] Mear's discipleship group that bright joined in 1947 while on campus; "Bill Bright," Christianity Today, Accessed July 27, 2021, Https://Www.Christianitytoday.Com/Ct/1997/July14/Bill-Brights-Wonderful-Plan-For-World.Html.

[58] John G. Turner, *Bill Bright and Campus Crusade for Christ: The Renewal of Evangelicalism in Postwar America*, First Edition. (Chapel Hill: The University of North Carolina Press, 2008), 18.

[59] Turner, *Bill Bright and Campus Crusade for Christ*, 18.

to serve inner cities, the military, athletes, political and business leaders, the entertainment industries, and families."[60]

Intervarsity Christian Fellowship

Charles Troutman (1914-1990), general director of Intervarsity Christian Fellowship (IVCF), said that "there is no place like the university for the sharpening and expansion of the Christian faith."[61] IVCF officially began in 1940. A document from 1942-43 showed an early imbalance between campuses and full-time staff with only eight staff to over 120 campuses, signifying an explosion on campus. Student initiative was the highlight of IVCF such that at one point, the staff was trying to catch up with the students' exponential growth.

IVCF held its first foreign missions conference with 300 students pledged to serve overseas. These conferences later became known as URBANA conferences. IVCF learned Scripture reading using the Inductive Bible study method, commitment to prayer and conducted Campus in the Woods, which became their annual, month-long training at a camp. Many students who came to the first Campus in the Woods became vital leaders in the IVCF.

After seventy-five years of campus ministry, IVCF is present on over 700 college campuses mirroring their long-term mantra, "Change the university. Change the world."[62]

Student Church Planting Experience

Jaeson Ma, the author of *The Blueprint,* shares equal intentionality about evangelizing college students. As the director of Campus Church Networks in his early twenties, he developed a model using the campus as a church planting strategy. His ministry planted more than 300 student-led house churches in North America and East Asia. He combined prayer groups and campus ministries as strategic ways to start a church. In the latter part of his book, he mentioned that most of the students who became new believers "did not fit into Christian fellowships that have already existed because they were culturally or socially different."[63] Campus Church Network dissolved in 2010 and merged with Student Church, founded by Erik Fish. It is a church planting movement, empowering students to start a campus church anywhere around the globe.

---

[60] "Bill Bright | Cru," Cru, accessed January 1, 2020, https://www.cru.org/us/en/about/billbright/profile.html.

[61] Hunt, Keith, and Gladys Hunt. *For Christ and the University: The Story of InterVarsity Christian Fellowship of the USA - 1940-1990.* (Downers Grove, Ill: IVP Books, 1992) 2.

[62] "InterVarsity," accessed July 27, 2021, https://intervarsity.org/.

[63] Jaeson Ma and Lou Engle, *The Blueprint: A Revolutionary Plan to Plant Missional Communities on Campus* (Ventura, CA: Regal Books, 2007), 201.

Every Nation Ministries

Steve and Deborah Murrell were part of an American missions team that came to the Philippines in the 1980s when the Philippines was in political turmoil and economic catastrophe. Daily protests by students prevailed during those times.

During that one-month outreach,

180 Filipinos converted to Christianity through open-air preaching, rock and roll seminar and arts right at the heart of University Belt in 1984. It gradually grew into a multi-site, multi-generational, Christ-centered, Spirit-empowered, socially-responsible church that meets in sixteen different locations in Metro Manila. Since then, Victory Philippines multiplied to sixty different cities, sent and funded Filipinos cross-culturally to over half a dozen nations, including China, UAE, Bangladesh, Nepal, Vietnam, Cambodia, and others.[64]

Victory Philippines started as a small group of Filipino students that turned into a vibrant and growing campus ministry and churches in the Philippines and influenced other nations. Every Nation Ministries continues to thrive in its global presence in eighty-two nations.[65]

Campus Ministry has always been at the forefront of Every Nation Ministries. Jun Escosar, President of Every Nation Seminary, is one of the first few students who became a Christian in the 1980s when American college students went to the Philippines for an outreach. As a college student himself at the time of his conversion, he continues to understand and live out this value. When Victory University Belt began in 1984, it was mainly composed of Filipino students from low-income families in the provinces who moved to Manila to pursue education. University Belt has the highest concentration of students coming from across the nation. The brightest of the land converge here. It has been a battleground of government protests for many years as the *Malacanang*[66] resides there.

Escosar emphasized a chapter in his book, *A Bible and A Passport, Why Every Nation Ministries Values Campus and Why It Must Be Church-Based*. Church-based campus ministries are not as popular nor the same thing as having a campus ministry "on the sideline.". Escosar further explained how one rarely finds a local church that began as a campus ministry and has maintained an ongoing and effective impact on the campus. Moreover, if you look for a worldwide movement of churches with a mission to both the community and

---

[64] Steve Murrell, *100 Years From Now: Sustaining a Movement for Generations*, 1st Edition. (Nashville, TN: Dunham Books, 2013), 13.

[65] "Every Nation Global Family of Churches," accessed December 8, 2020, https://www.everynation.org.

[66] *Malacanang* is where the President of the Philippines resides. It is the counterpart of The White House in the United States.

university campuses, you will find few examples.[67] Every Nation Ministries has continued to embrace the tension of being a church-based campus ministry since its founding in 1994.

Below are a few examples from Every Nation Ministries of church-based campus ministry engagement from Escosar's accounts in his book, *A Bible and A Passport*.

Grace Bible Church Pearlside, Honolulu, Hawaii

Pearlside was planted by Norman Nakanishi in 1994 and established Every Nation Campus in Hawaii. It has four active campus ministries in four universities on the island of Oahu. The church's steady increase is directly related to its persistent outreach in the universities. Norman Nakanishi is well known for his remark, "this is not their campus ministry; it is *our* (italics mine) campus ministry." He embraced the tension of working as a pastor for both the church and campus. Managing this tension provided growth to the church long-term.

Every Nation Stellenbosch, Western Cape, South Africa

Reaching the students from the University of Stellenbosch in 1994 birthed EN Stellenbosch. Escosar describes the campus engagment:

> The campus ministry currently has over 100 student-led connect groups and over 800 students attending their campus services. The focus is on equipping and releasing students to lead. Its campus ministry has also raised many student government leaders who have served within the university organization and structure.[68]

Rice Brooks, co-founder of Every Nation Ministries, for years evangelized mainly in the universities, conversing with students from agnostics, atheists, and all kinds of spiritual backgrounds. Once, he conducted a *God's Not Dead* event in Bolivia, which filled the auditorium, leaving hundreds of students hungry for more of God's revelation.

In the United States, Seth Trimmer from Corvallis, OR, and Adam Mabry from Cambridge, MA, managed church-based campus ministry tensions. Both churchs' proximity to universities has proved a gateway to students. The vibrancy of college students within their corresponding churches is contagious.

These campus ministries demonstrated their impact on missions, student leadership development, church planting, and the importance of a church-based campus ministry organization.

International Student Ministries, a Step Closer to Missions.

---

[67] Dr Jun Escosar and Walter Walker, *A Bible and a Passport: Obeying the Call to Make Disciples in Every Nation* (Every Nation Productions, 2019), kindle loc 5042.

[68] Escosar and Walker, kindle loc 5216.

The global north hosts the top five receiving countries of international students. These countries are the United States, United Kingdom, Australia, France, and Germany.[69] The economic value that international students bring to the United States alone is remarkable. One-quarter of the founders of the One-billion-dollar start-up companies first came to America as international students.[70]

The United States, as stated earlier, is the number one hosting country for international students. The State Department lists "nearly 300 world leaders, current and former, who chose US institutions, a trend that analysts say reinforced the nation's status as the global leader in higher education."[71] These international students are excellent, *crème* of the crop, highly motivated individuals. Their country sends the best of their students with the hope of bringing back to their country fundamentals that would contribute to their nation's economy or policies.

Inevitably, most of them held on to their ancestors' beliefs and religion until they came to America. Like Kay, she held on to her Buddha necklace from childhood until her baptism day. These international students are mostly coming from the 10/40 window. Roots of eastern religions such as Buddhism and Hinduism reside in these countries. However, that is also changing. The top three countries of origin of international students are China, India, and South Korea.[72] All these three countries currently belong to the largest Christian communities globally, as stated by Jenkins. South Korea is one of the largest missionary-sending countries to date. China's underground Christian churches and house churches are continuously multiplying. The Philippines, which is also part of the 10/40 window, is believed to take the place of the fourth largest Christian community on the planet by 2050. We are not just looking at ministering to international students as an opportunity to reach those who belong to the unevangelized, but they are coming in as missionaries and church planters in the global north, a perfect example of glocalized missions. We are indeed experiencing a reverse mission that is polycentric and multi-directional.

One example is the life of Lisa Espineli Chinn, who was born and raised in the Philippines. Lisa is the first female International Student Director of Intervarsity Christian Fellowship. As an international student at Wheaton Graduate School then, she was connected immediately to Intervarsity USA. She

[69] Russell King, Allan Findlay, Jill Ahrnes, "International Student Mobility Literature," Bristol, Higher Education Funding Council for England, Research Gate, accessed February 24, 2020, https://www.researchgate.net/figure/Top-ten-host-countries-for-international-students-global-total-and-UK-origin-students.

[70] Stuart Anderson, "National Foundation for American Policy," accessed January 1, 2020, https://nfap.com.

[71] "World Leaders Study in the United States," Homeland Security, accessed March 12, 2020, https://studyinthestates.dhs.gov/2012/11/world-leaders-study-in-the-united-states.

[72] Youyou Zhou, "The Impact of Chinese Students in the US, Charted and Mapped," Quartz, accessed March 6, 2019, https://qz.com/1410768/the-number-of-chinese-students-in-the-us-charted-and-mapped.

initially served as a student volunteer on campus and later became an Intervarsity staff. Her mission engagement was multilevel, from hospitality, mentorship, and mobilization, to creating ministry models, equipping intercultural competency within and outside her organization, and spearheaded pioneering projects. Some of the projects she implemented are International Students Track at Urbana, Internationals for God's Kingdom (INK) conferences—addressing reentry issues, and I-GIG (Groups Investigating God)—where she assembled a team of Bible study writers to create a Bible study material for both Americans and international students. Lisa published books *Think Home, Back Home, Coming to America/Returning Home to Your Country.* In 2010, she was awarded the prestigious Hugh Jenkins Award for Excellence in Community Programming by NAFSA.[73] She was the ambassador for the whole Intervarsity movement and put ISM on the Intervarsity map.[74] For Lisa, her ministry involvement with Intervarsity includes practicing hospitality, introducing other Americans and internationals to her culture, in love and acceptance. She offered one of her strengths as a Filipino by acting as a host to a foreign country. Lisa exemplified an international leader, that even though she came in as a foreigner in a country, she still acted as a host and became a blessing to others.

Lisa's life story is yet another example of diaspora mission and glocalization—truly multi-directional and polycentric. ISM sees the nations within our borders as missions at our doorstep.

Intercultural Campus Ministry values missions across the globe and missions within the borders. In chapter four, the convergence is further explained and illustrated.

Relational Realism

Diaspora missions is the contemporary missiological response to the new realities we face in the current globalization, and the relational realism paradigm is the most compatible mission practice for scattered missionaries who mainly originate from the majority world. "The changing landscape of the 21st century, namely, the global phenomena of large-scale diaspora and Christendom's shifting center of gravity, requires serious reflections on the missiological conceptualizations and strategies for Christian missions."[75]

Shane Mikeska outlined relational realism by first critiquing Paul Heibert's Critical Realism.[76]

---

[73] NAFSA is the world's largest non-profit association dedicated to International Educators.

[74] Stacey Beiler and Lisa Espinelli Chinn, "History of International Student Ministry in Intervarsity/USA in Wan et al., *Diaspora Missions to International Students*, 103–112.

[75] Wan, *Diaspora Missiology*, 3.

[76] See Paul Heibert's work on *Missiological Implications of Epistemological Shifts: Affirming Truth in Modern/Postmodern World.*

Historically, critical realism emerged out of the tension between modernism and post-modernism; epistemologically, critical realism espoused a 1:1 correlation between human perception and reality, i.e., the world could be observed, experimented upon, and fully understood through scientific method...in scientific inquiry, this epistemology is labeled 'positivism.' Critical realism affirms that reality or truth can be observed and described by humans.[77]

Mikeska proceeded to contrast that with relational realism,

... man was created in the image of God and his existence (ontologically) is solely dependent on God at all times (Gen.1:26-27, Rom.11:36; Heb.1:3). His ability to know (epistemologically) and his undertaking in missions (*missio Dei*) are all dependent on God, who is the Great "I AM" (Exo.3).[78]

The relational realism paradigm posits that "reality is based on relationships between created beings and the Creator. God's purpose is relational. Our calling in mission is relational and training for mission also needs to be relational."[79] This can be traced back to Enoch Wan's article on "Relational Theology and Relational Missiology."[80] He defines the paradgigm as such:

Ontologically, 'relational realism' is to be defined as the systematic understanding that 'reality' is primarily based on the 'vertical relationship' between God and the created order and secondarily 'horizontal relationship' within the created order.[81]

---

[77] "Enoch Wan and Shane Mikeska, *Engaging the Secular World through Life-on-Life Disciple-Making in the British Context: Relational Paradigm in Action* (Relational Series Book 1) (Portland OR: Western Seminary Press, 2019), 27.

[78] Wan and Mikeska, *Engaging the Secular World through Life-on-Life Disciple-Making in the British Context*, 28.

[79] Wan and Hedinger, *Relational Missionary Training*, 14.

[80] Enoch Wan, "Relational Theology and Relational Missiology," EMS occasional Bulletin, Vol. 21 No.1, PDF.

[81] Wan and Hedinger, *Relational Missionary Training*, 17.

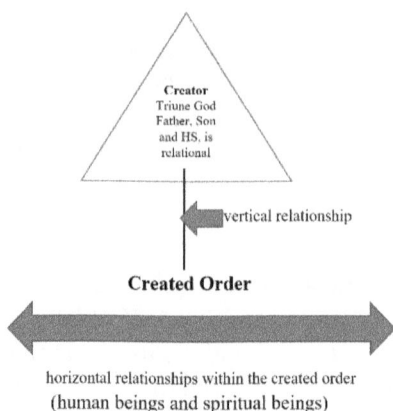

Figure 1 Relational Realism Diagram at the Macro Level

Wan and Hedinger state that, Missions is about "human beings who are in a relationship with God introducing yet another human being to Him."[82] Several publications[83] support this theory preceding the release of the book *Relational Missionary Training* by Wan and Hedinger.

The first order in understanding our relationship with others is to understand the relationships at work within the Trinity. We look at the trinitarian relationships to model or pattern after our relationships with others. Theologian Peter Leithart explained two concepts of Trinitarian relationships, "immanent" and "economic." The former refers to the intra-trinitarian relationship that is exclusive and eternal; the latter refers to the Trinitarian relationships revealed within the history of Jesus Christ. It is "God's administration of salvation. It is the economy of redemption."[84] To echo Leithart, Horrell, Wan, and Hedinger, the economic Trinity is an accurate representation but not the complete and totality of God. Leithart explains the doctrine of the Trinity as a practical doctrine:

> It tells us what God is like, it tells us what we are to be like, it says something about the kind of God that we worship, and the way God interacts with us and with the world. As we understand more and more what the Bible reveals to us about the Father, Son, and Holy Spirit, the more practical the doctrine becomes (Leithart, 2016).

---

[82] Wan and Hedinger, *Relational Missionary Training*, 17.

[83] See articles by Enoch Wan on,"The Paradigm of Relational Realism", "Relational Theology and Relational Missiology", and "Relational Study of the Trinity and the Epistle to the Philippians."

[84] Peter J. Leithart, *Th215 Trinitarian Theology*, Logos Class (Bellingham, Wa: Lexham Press, 2016)

Triune God is Relational

Here are three Immanent Trinitarian Concepts explained by Leithart on Trinitarian Theology:[85]

Table 1 Immanent Trinitarian Concepts by Leithart

The Father Eternally Begets the Son	Regardless of whether the Son entered the world in the incarnation or whether there was a world for him to enter in the first place, the Father eternally begets the Son. This is true even if the world had never existed.
The Son Eternally Loves the Father	The Son eternally loves the Father, not when he incarnated not after the resurrection, but the Son eternally loves the Father.
The Spirit Eternally Proceeds	The Holy Spirit eternally binds the Father and the Son, whether we take the Eastern view of the Holy Spirit proceeds from the Father through the son or the western view where the Holy Spirit proceeds from the Father and the Son, the Spirit's relationship to the Father and Son is the same eternally.

The common word between these three ontological trinitarian concepts is the word "Eternal." Relationships within the Trinity existed even before the creation of the world. In other words, within the Trinity, *relationships are eternal*.

Another compelling element in immanent Trinity is that the three are personal Beings. Wan and Hedinger explain:

> These are neither simple forces nor manifestations of one another. They are truly personal beings, distinct from one another and yet intimately, dynamically related as well. The personal nature of the relationships between the members of the Trinity led Horrel to write that the three members of the Godhead are 'genuinely personal in relationships.[86]

---

85 Peter J. Leithart, *Th215 Trinitarian Theology*.
86 Wan and Hedinger, *Relational Missionary Training*, 28.

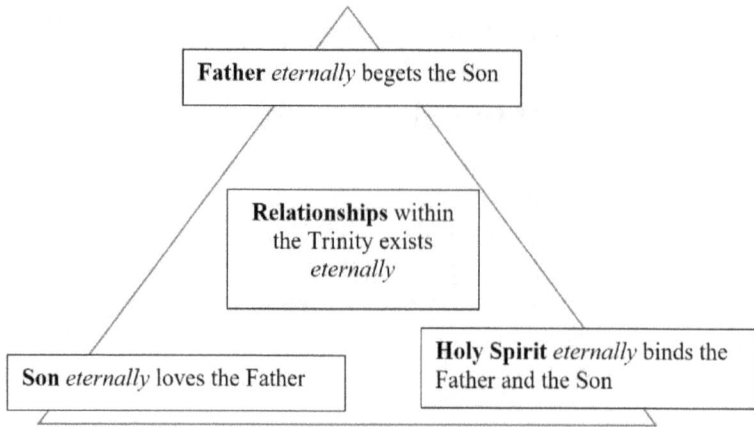

Figure 2 Immanent Relationships Within the Trinity

In his classic systematic theology, Wan and Hedinger then refer to William Shedd regarding how the personal beings relate to one another.[87] His answer led us to the following Scriptures:

Table 2 Members of the Trinity Relate to One Another by William Shedd[88]

John 3:35	One person loves one another
John 14:10,11	Persons dwell in one another
Zech. 13:7	One person suffers for one another
Matt. 11:27	One person knows another
Heb. 1:8	Person addresses one another
John 14:6	One person is the way to another
Luke 3:22	One person speaks of another
John 17:5	One person glorifies another
Gen. 1:26, 11:7	The persons confer with one another
Isa. 9:6	The persons make plans with one another
Gen.16:7, John 14:26	One person sends another
Phil. 2:5-11, Heb. 2:9	One person rewards another

---

[87] Wan and Hedinger, *Relational Missionary Training*, 28.
[88] Wan and Hedinger, *Relational Missionary Training*, 28-29.

The three, Father, Son, and Holy Spirit are distinct from one another, doing things of God in each role and maintaining their deity.

The economic Trinity refers to "God's administration of salvation. It is the economy of redemption. It is the Trinity revealed within the history of Jesus Christ"[89]. Here are the two Economic Trinitarian concepts by Leithart on Trinitarian Theology[90]

Table 3 Economic Trinitarian Concepts by Leithart

The Father sent the Son	In order for the Father to send the Son into the world, the world has to be created first.
The Spirit is poured out	The Spirit poured out on the day of Pentecost to the disciples.

Freidrich Hegel, a German philosopher, proposed that God's triune nature was revealed throughout history or that God progressively realizes Himself to be triune. However, the Orthodox Trinitarian in the early church, Middle Ages, and the Reformation era all agreed that God is eternally triune.[91]

Leithart explains why our understanding of the Triune God is integral to the Gospel. Leithart narrates the following points:[92]

a) God must save us. Man cannot save himself. God cannot send a subordinate to save us.

b) God must also send equal power and authority to preach the message of the good news. The transformative power of the Gospel, restoration of man's relationship to God, and bringing *shalom,* rely on the power of the Holy Spirit.

> The saving message of the gospel needs to be heard and believed, and God does not delegate the task of making sure that the Word is heard and believed to some subordinate. Of course, human beings proclaim the gospel, human beings evangelize; but it's the Spirit of God who ensures that the message has power unto salvation. It is the Spirit of God that ensures that those who hear the message believe the message. It is not simply that the Father sent the Son, and then human beings proclaimed the good news of the Son. God Himself takes on the task, not only saving us, but also ensuring that the saving message is heard and believed so that all nations might know that Jesus Christ is Lord and all of them might bow their knee to Him.[93]

---

[89] Peter Leithart, *Th215 Trinitarian Theology.*

[90] Peter Leithart, *Th215 Trinitarian Theology.*

[91] Peter Leithart, *Th215 Triniatrian Theology.*

[92] Peter Leithart, *Th215 Triniatrian Theology.*

[93] Peter Leithart, *Th215 Trinitarian Theology*

c) The savior must be God and the one who ensures the transformative message must be God. God takes many forms as he desires to reveal himself (i.e., dreams, spiritual encounters, human encounters).

d) Salvation is coming to know God. John 17:3 "Now this is eternal life: that they know you, the only true God, and Jesus Christ, whom you have sent" (New International Version). Eternal life is to know God through Christ. The good news is that the God who created us, pursued and saved us. His mission, His way, His method, His glory. Therefore, to go and make disciples is to make Christ known, as mentioned in Ephesians chapter three.

e) The message of the gospel is a Trinitarian message. If there is no Trinity, Christ is no God and there will be no revelation of God.

> "If the Holy Spirit be not God, then the love and self-communication of God to the human soul are not a reality. In other words, "without the doctrine of the Trinity we go back to mere natural religion and far off God"[94]

God Desires Relationships with His Created Beings

The previous section provides numerous accounts from scholars who emphasized that Triune God is relational, the importance of understanding the relational aspects of the Trinity, and how it relates to our understanding of salvation and His mission. The following section will explore the second relational element in relational realism paradigm: the vertical relationship between God and His created beings.

Genesis 1 is fundamental to our identity and calling. "So God created mankind in his own image, in the image of God he created them; male and female he created them" (Gen. 1:26-27, New English Translation). He established who we are (identity) and what we are called to do (calling/purpose) in the context of community or relationship with another, male and female; he created them. As created in God's image, our identity and purpose are interconnected; both are timeless and encompassing. It transcends peoples of every nation, tribe, and language throughout time because it is an *extension of His character* as our Triune God who is relational. However, in Genesis 3, the direct access was broken when "they hid from the LORD in the garden" (Gen 3:8, New English Translation). In this case, humans exchanged their identity and calling to image God to self-definition of identity and calling. Jesus came and restored that. The book of Hebrews testifies,

> After God spoke long ago in various portions and in various ways to our ancestors through the prophets, in these last days, he has spoken to us in a son, whom he appointed heir of all things, and through whom he created the

---

[94] Augustus Hopkins Strong, *Systematic Theology* (Philadelphia: American Baptist Publication Society, 1907), 349.

world. The Son is the radiance of his glory and the representation of his essence, and he sustains all things by his powerful word, and so when he had accomplished cleansing for sins, he sat down at the right hand of the Majesty on high. Thus he became so far better than the angels as he has inherited a name superior to theirs. (Heb 1: 1-4, New English Translation).

Jesus Christ is the radiance of God's glory and representation of his essence; his crucifixion and resurrection restored humanity's calling and identity. The Gospel of Matthew asserts that he restored all authority in heaven and on earth and has given his disciples an extension of that restored authority to make disciples of all nations (Matt 28: 18-20). Humanity's calling and identity to image God is possible through His Son Jesus Christ by the power of the Holy Spirit. Jesus made it possible for us, as Paul addressed the church in Philippi, to be united in Christ, to have the same mindset as Christ Jesus (Phil 2).

The kind of relationship our Triune God desires is the one that reflects and image a relational God. It is a biblical principle for healthy, godly relationships. The famous great commission, "Go and make disciples of all nations," is to live as created in God's image in the context of community.

The diagram below is meant to encapsulate the primary points I have laid out above.

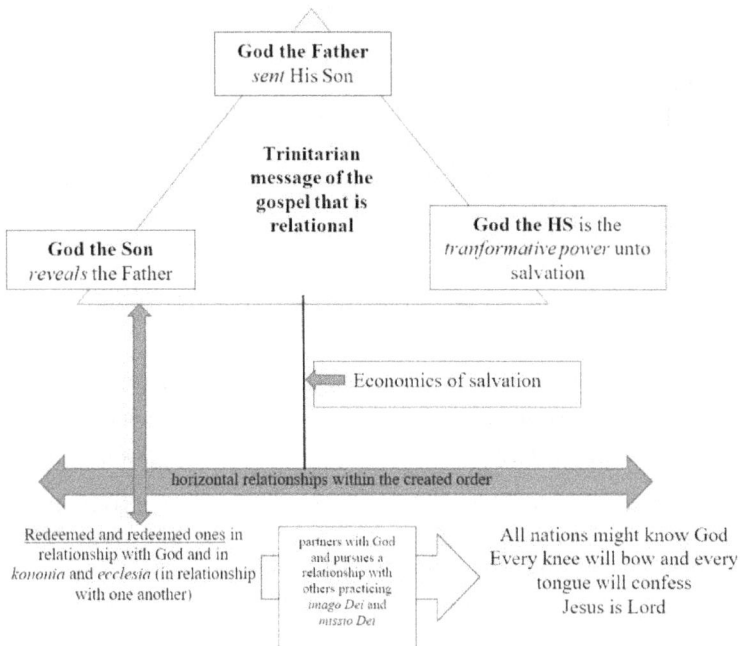

Figure 3 Trinitarian Message of the Gospel

One of the most compelling stories on relationships from the Bible is in 1 Corinthians 11:23-26. It is also the most familiar passage used in church during communion.

> For I received from the Lord what I also passed on to you: The Lord Jesus, on the night he was betrayed, took bread, and when he had given thanks, he broke it and said, "This is my body, which is for you; do this in remembrance of me." In the same way, after supper he took the cup, saying, "This cup is the new covenant in my blood; do this, whenever you drink it, in remembrance of me." For whenever you eat this bread and drink this cup, you proclaim the Lord's death until he comes (New International Version).

The Last Supper displays the Father's love and relationship at the very moment of our abandonment of Him. God entered into a covenant relationship with his created beings at the height of the disciples' betrayal and cowardice. Such a remarkable display of love and relationships not just to his followers but to those who are his enemies. Morris says it well: "Paul brings out the poignant truth that that feast of love that was to bring such strength and consolation to Christians was instituted at the very time when human malignancy was engaged in betraying the Saviour to his enemies."[95]

Wan and Hedinger survey the Scripture confirming God's desire for healthy relationship:[96]

a) Deuteronomy 6:5, "Love the Lord your God will all your heart and with all your soul and with all your strength" (New International Version).

b) Prophet's call for a relational depth in Jeremiah 9:23-24 "...let him who boasts boast about this, that he understands and knows me, that I am the Lord who exercises kindness, justice and righteousness on earth, for these I delight" (New International Version).

c) Micah spoke against cold, religious formalism that neglects what God seeks, "To act justly, love mercy and walk humbly with God" (Micah 6:8b, New International Version).

Other scholars assert the reality of God's relationality towards His creation. Tozer wrote, "Essentially salvation is the restoration of a right relation between man and his Creator, a bringing back to normal of the Creator-creation relation."[97] On the topic of relational ministry, Shane Mikeska expounds that,

> God invites us into His fellowship, as humans are created to be in a unique relationship with the Creator. The horizontal reconciliation in Ephesians of age, class, gender, and race comprises the love your neighbor

---

[95] Morris, L. (1985). *1 Corinthians: An Introduction and Commentary* (Vol. 7, p. 157). Downers Grove, IL: InterVarsity Press.

[96] Wan and Hedinger, *Relational Missionary Training*, 30-31.

[97] A.W. Tozer, *The Pursuit of God*, Kindle loc, 38.

commandment, which is a mere reflection of the greatest commandment: the vertical reconciliation of sinners to God (Eph. 2:1-10).[98]

Steve Murrell wrote a section, "Discipleship is Relationship," in *WikiChurch* and defines discipleship as three relational components: "first with God (follow), then with nonbelievers (fish), and finally with God's people (fellowship)."[99] Plueddemann offers something akin to relational realism paradigm in his definition of leadership. He values reflective mentoring in godly leadership development to promote God's ultimate purpose for the individual to enter into a relationship with their creator.[100]

Reese and Loane argue that leadership in churches, "for the last fifty years, has been functionalized and depersonalized into programs that have steadily eroded the very core of Christian life, which ought to be a life trinitarian-shaped intimacy and community."[101]

For Reese and Loane,

"Mentoring is simply paying attention and joining to what God has already been doing in people's lives. The way to do this is by coming alongside others as a guide and a friend. Sadly, many well-intended servants of the Lord are driven to get things done for God; they neglect both themselves and the people they serve. It is no wonder that many followers of Jesus today feel as though they have been reduced to 'functionaries for God' as James Houston puts it, 'How can I get more people to do more?'[102]

The authors of *Deep Mentoring* acknowledge the baggage of leadership built over the years and are now proposing a different idea. First, mentoring is *noticing the ones around you*. Secondly, it is *walking alongside others* who want to grow in maturity while discerning what God is already doing in their lives. This type of mentoring is deep, slow in the process, and unhurried. While the authors believed that God is still in the business of appointing, developing, or raising leaders to carry out His purposes here on earth, it made the strong point that discipleship is the first order of business before making immediate strategic plans for leadership formation.

J. Lee Grady wrote when invited to speak at mass evangelism events: "I am not against mass evangelism. I am not criticizing people who organize big

---

[98] Wan and Mikeska, *Engaging the Secular World through Life-on-Life Disciple-Making in the British Context,* 30.

[99] Steve Murrell, *WikiChurch: Making Discipleship Engaging, Empowering, and Viral,* Illustrated edition. (Lake Mary, Fla: Charisma House, 2011), 69.

[100] James Plueddemann, *Leading Across Cultures: Effective Ministry and Mission in the Global Church* (Downers Grove, IL: InterVarsity Press,2009), 158-159.

[101] Randy D. Reese, Robert Loane, and Eugene Peterson, *Deep Mentoring: Guiding Others on Their Leadership Journey* (IVP Books, 2012), kindle loc. 70.

[102] Reese, Loane and Peterson, *Deep Mentoring,* kindle, loc. 152.

meetings. However, I am learning that the best way to impact a large number of people is to focus on a few."[103] Grady further mentioned that

> Jesus calls us to do ministry His way—by making disciples. Yet in today's performance-based culture, we think bigger is better. We put all our money and time into splashy events while ignoring relationships. We want the sensational, not the simple. We crave big meetings, bigger platforms, noisy sermons, hyped-up altar calls, and instant results. It may look spectacular on opening night, but the show fades fast.[104]

How might the above relate to on-the-ground realities in campus ministry? Every year, different campus ministries are invited during the Freshmen week at the University of Washington to set up booths and tables to invite students to a religious club. Others opted out for a more grandiose set-up, like a taco truck giving free meals all day, popcorn and slushie machines, tickets to concert nights, ipads, and the like—anything extravagant just to attract students. However, my conversations with some of the campus ministers from other campus ministries reveal that they too, are not buying it. They are exhausted with such methods, emotionally and spiritually. It simply is not life-giving. It drains the minister. Grady concluded his statement with this,

> Leaders all around the world are coming to this same conclusion. They recognize that today's fatherless generation is looking for more than the hottest music, the coolest stage lighting, or the hippest techno-pastor. They want authentic role models who will spend time with them.[105]

If we want to understand life, we must understand the relationship, and if we want to understand the relationship, we must understand it from the relational God. Therefore, our calling in life and missions is, first and foremost, relational.[106]

Summary

As migration reached an all-time high of 272 million international migrants worldwide, these global phenomena and Christendom's shift from Europe to the Majority World require deep reflections on our understanding and undertaking of Christian missions. Diaspora missions is the contemporary missiological response to the new realities we face in the current globalization. Relational realism paradigm is the most compatible mission practice or framework for scattered missionaries who mainly originate from the Majority World. Intercultural campus ministry, a convergence of campus ministry and

---

[103] J. Lee Grady, "Why Relational Discipleship Has Become My Priority," Charisma News, accessed February 2, 2021, https://www.charismanews.com/opinion/33499-why-relational-discipleship-has-become-my-priority.

[104] Grady, "Why Relational Discipleship Has Become My Priority."

[105] Grady, "Why Relational Discipleship Has Become My Priority."

[106] Wan and Hedinger, *Relational Missionary Training*, 19.

international student ministry, is a diaspora mission practice engaging both the local and the international students for global missions.

CHAPTER 3

GETTING TO KNOW THE PARTICIPANTS

Introduction

"Wear the Right Jacket"

It was wintertime when I officially moved from the Philippines to Seattle. Before Seattle, I had never been in bitterly cold weather before. The coldest weather we have in the Philippines is twenty degrees Celsius. The average weather in Seattle during February is between thirty to fifty degrees Fahrenheit or ten degrees Celsius. Even if I converted reading Fahrenheit to Celsius, I had no prior experience of what that piece of information means. Every time I stepped out of the house to go to campus, do my groceries or attend staff meetings, I was freezing. One time, I called one of the church staff to pick me up at my bus stop, which was just less than a mile away from our church office. I was too cold to walk the rest. Upon entering the room that morning for the staff meeting, the concerned look on their faces suggested something was off. Finally, one spoke up and said, "you are wearing the wrong jacket." I fondly recall this story now as I listen to the participants' emphatic reminder to future first-generation Filipino missionaries who will be serving in the global north: "Wear the right jacket!"

This chapter will present findings from Ria's dissertation. Themes emerged through a process of concept mapping, classifying of emerging themes based on three restraining forces (psychological, physical, and group culture,) coalescence of the restraining and driving forces, and finally the formation of conclusive statements.

Seven first-generation Filipino missionaries participated in Ria's study. These missionaries are based in Australia, Belgium, Canada, Germany, London, and Ukraine. Each participant received the questions before the scheduled interview, and each interview lasted ninety minutes. The style of inquiry patterned after Patton's classification of interviews[107] is both structured and conversational. Let us get to know our participants.

Question No. 1 Briefly Share How You Became a Follower of Christ.

It is Not Enough to Have a Religious Background.

The majority of the participants came from a nominal Catholic background or religious background. How they came to know the Lord was due to a close

---

[107] Johnson and Christensen, *Educational Research*, 236.

encounter with one of their close friends, a best friend, a classmate, or a roommate who followed Christ after experiencing the transformative power of the gospel. These life-changing transformations were people they knew who were once depressed, enslaved in drug addiction, or lived a destructive lifestyle. A group of students invited them to a Christian gathering. They noticed that they exude the same joy, peace, and an attractive perspective in life. It was not hard for them to attend a Christian gathering since they modeled a strong sense of community and radically transformed lives. For students who mostly come from low-income families, joyfulness amidst hardship is extraordinary. The message of the Good News is becoming evident in their lives even through hard life circumstances.

Most participants became part of the community before fully surrendering their lives to Christ. During this time, they served in churches as volunteers in different ministries as ushers/greeters by providing administration help. They joined Bible study groups and were discipled through what they call "small groups." It is also important to point out that aside from these transformed lives and a strong sense of community, these participants indicated that they can still vividly remember the first time they attended church. The whole experience was memorable; the worshipful experience, "cut-to-the-heart" preaching, and a vibrant young community, mostly students or young families living their lives for Christ in such a radical, contagious for Christ lifestyle. Having a Catholic and religious background somehow did not answer their need to be discipled and follow Christ. These needs were met when they became part of a discipleship group or small group.

Question No. 2 How Did You Become a Part of a Church in the Global North?

"No More Land to Conquer."

Calling is the central umbrella of how the participants ended up as a missionary in the global north. For one, it was after participating in a mission trip to Latvia. One family was interceding for a friend in Ukraine during the war in 2014. Two missionaries realized they were being called to their contexts after several visits to the city, visiting financial partners and relatives. The other two missionaries in the Philippines met their husbands at a world conference and joined their new husbands' ministry in the global north. All the participants have been in ministry as full-time staff from the Philippines for at least ten years, to which three of the participants said, "I have maximized my time in the Philippines." One added, "there are no more new lands to conquer."[108] After knowing the need in Europe, one cannot help but respond. It

---

[108] At the time, there are over 300 campus missionaries in the Philippines and only two in Every Nation London.

pained her to see the rich heritage of Christianity in her city, yet it was just part of history for them.

All participants have been a full-time staff for ten to almost thirty years. None of them had major problems with visa acquisition. Four of the participants received their citizenship through marriage. One initially came in as an international student with a full scholarship at a university to study their language. Of all the transitions they needed to navigate, acquiring a visa was the least troublesome.

Questions No. 3 Which of the Three-Fold Focus of Ministry Did You Start?

"Reaching These Postmodern Students With the Gospel Will Change the Narratives of the Future."

Every Nation family of churches is known for its three-fold focus, campus ministry, world missions, and church planting.[109] One participant said that his focus has always been church planting back then (Philippines) and globally. He planted five new churches through his Filipino connections in his first two years as a church planter in the global north. He believes that his specific calling is to "reach Filipinos first, to reach the nations." His strategy is to "Organize, Strategize, Mobilize." He strongly prefers planting a new church with Filipinos because of their "trust and generosity," which he emphasized are essential in church planting. When planting a church, he decided to adopt a more global name, Every Nation, rather than Victory (Philippines' church name) to be a church for other nationalities. It was a paradigm shift for him, who used to pastor a monocultural church for decades in the Philippines, to pastor a church in the global north. This church was primarily Filipino and is slowly transitioning toward interculturalism, as Filipinos in interracial marriages bring their spouses to church. It is a paradigm shift for Filipino missionaries to lead from a monocultural church to an intercultural church, and strategically use the global name Every Nation which creates leverage for the church to be inclusive of other nationalities.

When asked which three-fold focus they find themselves more involved in, all participants unanimously said, "they overlap and are interconnected." The participants find themselves on a mission, reaching the next generation in church planting initiatives. They minister to students and young families. Reaching the next generation is at the forefront of their participation in missions or church planting. Some participants strategically picked a church location accessible to universities, a trend common among Every Nation Global Family of Churches. One emphasized how vital reaching the next generation is. He said, "reaching these postmodern students with the gospel will change the

---

[109] "Every Nation Global Family of Churches, accessed January 1, 2020, https://www.everynation.org/.

narratives of the future."[110] This value can be traced back to when these participants first encountered Christ as students and how students are at the forefront of missions, church planting, and campus ministries.

Their heart and passion for missions were evident in their replies. One said this Bible verse is a quick reminder for her when missionary activities are discouraging: "One who wins soul is wise" (Proverbs 11:30, New International Version). She carried this verse when she was a missionary as a single woman, and continues to do so now. She and her husband are currently based in Germany and are part of the leadership team. She learned to manage a household with three kids, all under ten, and minister in a foreign country. She preached a few times in English, one form of ministry she does not hesitate to do if she has more free time from family responsibilities. Her pastor and church members commended her for preaching well.

Question No. 4 As a First-Generation Filipino Missionary in Your Context, What Stands Out in Your Mind?

"I am Bigger than my Background."

All the participants in my research unanimously perceived themselves as a blessing to many nations. Their faith is a testament of God's goodness in their lives in whatever circumstances. Holding on to the promise of God, "Ask me, and I will give your nations as an inheritance, the ends of the earth your possession" (Psalm 2:8, New International Version) resonates within their soul. Through discipleship, leadership development, and empowerment they received, their perception changed from self-pity mentality or *kawawa*, to "I am bigger than my background because I have a big God" mentality. One participant said, "at the end of the day, I know I am a child of God."[111] "I see myself how God sees me" is the identity that sustains them through the challenges as a missionary. Furthermore, the participants gained fresh eyes and new perspectives on missions in this new reality they find themselves in.

As a foreigner in their context, it also highlights the positive traits of Filipinos, such as joyfulness, boldness in sharing their faith, and high proficiency in English. They also perceived themselves as welcoming, non-threatening, adaptable, flexible, relational, and confident in re-shaping the culture. These positive Filipino traits and a strong sense of calling to these nations moved the participants to the global north, pioneer a campus ministry, join the local team, or start a new church.

However, these traits are not perceived entirely as positive by their host city. Most of them encountered locals questioning their joyfulness, mistaken as

---

[110] All interviews are confidential; the names of the interviewees are withheld by mutual agreement." Interviewed by Ria L. Martin. Seattle. March 30, 2021.

[111] All interviews are confidential; the names of the interviewees are withheld by mutual agreement." Interviewed by Ria L. Martin. Seattle. March 29, 2021

"something is wrong with you" or "what seems to be funny?" That joy created a certain kind of strangeness for the host city. Furthermore, one local church member advised a Filipino missionary to "smile less, especially in public." The locals think it is appropriate to smile in small gatherings where it is received as authentic, but it can be viewed as insincere in public. That feedback from a trusted friend and staff of the church was received well by this Filipino missionary.

"It is not Working Here."

The spiritual growth in Asia[112] and specifically of Victory Philippines was phenomenal. Rice Brooks, a co-founder of Every Nation Ministries, most famously referred to the event as the "Miracle in Manila."[113] The spiritual growth there is known among Every Nation Global Family of Churches. This phenomenon contributed to Filipinos going on missions to other nations, first to Asia, then to the global north. More than half of the participants in this research indicated that "I have reached my capacity in the Philippines," and going to nations outside of Asia is the next step. A few of them even referred to a prophetic message from a conference held in South Africa in 2016 "about Asians and Africans helping in Europe,"[114] a missionary trajectory similarly mentioned by historians Jenkins and Noll. However, this same confidence, the growth experienced in the Philippines, also pulls them to wondering, "why is it not working here?" Participants realized that "we cannot just copy and paste" what we had or learned in the Philippines, that now "we just have to figure things out."

The participants used the phrase "discipleship is relationship," a popular discipleship principle in the Philippines. It refers to a discipleship model or track known as the "Four E's." The Four Es are "1) engage the culture and community, 2) establish biblical foundations, 3) equip believers to minister, and 4) empower disciples to make disciples."[115] It is in their understanding that evangelism and discipleship begin by building a relationship. However, in the global north, they encountered questions unfamiliar in a monocultural context. For instance, how do you engage the community with cultures that value time and relationships differently? Two perceptions are at play here, the Filipino missionary's view of their host city and how their host city views them. What kind of relationship do they have with their host country? Are they perceived as immigrants, minorities, or missionaries? How does the host country perceive

---

[112] The spiritual growth in Asia is phenomenal. Several books were written to testify about this. Here are a few, *The Next Christendom* by Philip Jenkins and *Polycentric Missions* by Allen Yeh, and Diaspora Missions series books by Enoch Wan.

[113] Rice Broocks, *Every Nation In Our Generation: Recovering the Apostolic Mandate* (Lake Mary, Fla.: Brentwood, TN: Creation House, 2002), 35.

[114] "All interviews are confidential; the names of the interviewees are withheld by mutual agreement." Interviewed by Ria L. Martin. Seattle. March 31, 2021.

[115] Murrell, *WikiChurch*, 91.

each of those roles? Secondly, what kind of relationship are the Filipinos trying to establish with the host city, as friends, neighbors, or messengers of the Good News? Even though the Filipino missionaries believe in the principles of discipleship, they acknowledged their "lack of intercultural training and mentorship" in contextualizing these principles. Some responses were "I felt like I was left to survive or go home," "I have no one to bounce ideas with," and "No one showed me how to do it in my context." While some had the liberty to explore and try other discipleship methods, guidance was still needed.

However, one church planter who started with Filipinos did not have trouble starting a church with a group of Filipinos. For him, starting a church this way and minimizing cultural barriers allowed him to start smoothly and much faster. This is a prevalent church planting practice with its roots from McGavran's Homogenous Unit Principle (HUP)[116]. At one point, their church grew from zero to five new church plants in two years, gathering Filipinos from five different cities in the region. His relational skills as a Filipino helped him start churches steadily, but this relational aspect also led to unfortunate incidents creating a series of relational missteps and errors. Participating in this project made him realize his mistakes in the past and brought healing in the process. He would love to leave someday a positive legacy for future Filipino missionaries in the global north.

In terms of discipleship methodology, most participants realized "we cannot just copy/paste what we knew then (Philippines setting) to where we are now." However, it is worth mentioning that one family successfully moved into their context. She said the key was "multiple-anchorship." Multiple anchorship means having several supporters who can provide feedback on different aspects of being an intercultural missionary. It also means group mentoring.[117] Their family stayed and lived in the United States for ten years. After graduating from the School of World Missions, she married and lived in the United States, where her husband is originally from, forming a new community and attending a local church in the United States. This community became their prayer partners and support group. In the United States, they participated in a one-year program by Every Nation Ministries called "Life Year," wherein missionaries take their time to raise their financial partnership team, receive mentorship, plan for their missionary engagement in their new context and learn the language. This same church became their sending church. She felt supported by this church even after living in their new home for six years. Their mentors were former American missionaries in their context, and their time with them has always been insightful, helping them navigate several intercultural settings they encountered. During the Life Year program, she learned the basics of the new language and managed realistic expectations as a

---

[116] McGavran, Donald A. *Understanding Church Growth*. Wm. B. Eerdmans Publishing, 1990.

[117] Group mentoring is an innovative way to invite several individuals within the organization to mentor based on their skills sets. See Lois J. Zachary, *The Mentor's Guide: Facilitating Effective Learning Relationships*, 2 edition. (San Francisco: Jossey-Bass, 2011), 72.

missionary to another nation. It is to "learn the culture, love the people, and serve the community/church." As part of the strategic leadership team of the church, they are managing their intercultural relations well, knowing they have a prayer team and mentors through Life Year. She said, "living in the US prepared us to live in Ukraine."

Question No. 5 What are Some Unique Experiences of a First-Generation Filipino Missionary in the Global North?

"How can I Share the Gospel to a Wealthy Nation When I Come from a Place of Poverty?"

Their local church in the Philippines is known for its spiritual and numerical growth among the Every Nation Global Family of Churches. While this phenomenon contributed to Filipinos going on missions to other nations, this same phenomenon dampens their confidence in a way that most of the participants in this research said, "I do not want to be perceived as a know-it-all or expert in missions, I want to be a learner." All the participants have been in the ministry as volunteers or staff for at least ten years, where discipleship was modeled for them and where they saw thousands of Filipinos baptized and surrendered their lives to Christ. Some of these former high school and college students are now politicians, businessmen, missionaries, and influencers in their generation. They saw discipleship at work. It was transferrable and straightforward. What they experienced in the Philippines and hope to see in their new context are not the same. It is a process of unlearning and realigning. It could be discouraging at times, especially when they are assimilating, creating a home space, and building new friendships and community while simultaneously trying to be an effective minister of the gospel.

Their move to the global north heightened their perception of themselves both in positive and negative ways. Filipino missionaries are faced with this new reality, "How can I share the gospel to a wealthy nation when I come from a place of poverty?" A local church member advised one Filipina missionary to be "mindful of how she presents herself" to avoid her association as one of the looming gypsies in the area. The local church member added, "I do not want you to be pushed aside and looked down upon." There are many gypsies in the area, and they sometimes create trouble in the city by pickpocketing and stealing. One time, she encountered one of the gypsies and was surprised to find many similarities to a gypsy: her skin color, height (much shorter relative to the locals), and petiteness. Since then, she has made an extra effort not to be sloppy with her fashion statement in public. Change of image was a consistent theme for most of the participants. Another family missionary said, "they do not want to lose their effectivity" to minister to other nationalities or "be labeled and put in the box" as ministers only to Filipinos. Their city has one of the highest numbers of immigrants and international students. Since their arrival,

39

they have been intentional in becoming a missionary for all nations. The decision to live in an urban setting was also a missional move.

All the participants in this research joined an established church in the global north except one who planted a church in a diverse metropolitan city by reaching Filipinos first. His plan to start a church with Filipinos has been his game plan at the very beginning. During his transition, he noticed that three to five Filipino families were moving to this nation per month, and most of them were either leaders or members of the church in the Philippines. He saw this as an opportunity to start a church with Filipino diaspora. He knows the need to reach other nations, and his heart is with it, but he would assume that it will happen more organically since the church and community where he lives are already diverse. He confessed that the idea to move into another nation at his age was surprising. He was already a pastor for several years in the Philippines and lived quite contently there. He thinks that missions are for the younger generation who have the physical capacity to adjust to a new nation, raise a partnership team, travel, and whose words are "more eloquent" than mine and can adapt a new image. He said, "I have a strong Filipino accent, I dress a certain way, and I look very Filipino."[118] Even though he was pleased and content with his lifestyle and relational connections in the Philippines, he said, "I cannot say no to God's call in my life." He knows that by reaching Filipinos in his local context, the church will eventually reach other nationalities. Currently, he is the only full-time staff in the church he initiated eight years ago. The church is well attended by many dependent, trustworthy volunteers and generous Filipinos who help finance church operations and manage their worship gatherings. He said, "I cannot imagine planting a church in a new nation without a team I can trust,"[119] a crucial point in church planting. For him, Filipinos' trustworthiness and generosity are incomparable. Generosity among Filipinos is one of the consistent positive traits mentioned by the participants.

One of the sources of anxiety for the participants before becoming a full-time missionary was how to tell their family members. Filipinos have a common perception that missionaries are poor, have no stable income, and are unable to help families financially. Nevertheless, many of them can testify to God's provision over their lives and family members. Generosity among Filipinos is seen both in their new contexts and back home. Some Filipino missionaries still have partners from the Philippines who are supporting missionaries to London and Belgium. This is another paradigm shift in missions from before, when only the wealthy nations could participate. One Filipino missionary testified that despite the recent financial instability caused by the pandemic, her financial partner in the Philippines did not miss a single month to support her. For her, that is generosity found in the Bible, "In the midst of a very severe trial, their

---

[118] All interviews are confidential; the names of the interviewees are withheld by mutual agreement." Interviewed by Ria L. Martin. Seattle. March 30, 2021

[119] All interviews are confidential; the names of the interviewees are withheld by mutual agreement." Interviewed by Ria L. Martin. Seattle. March 30, 2021

overflowing joy and their extreme poverty welled up in rich generosity" (2 Cor 8:2, New International Version).

A lack of intercultural competency emerged during the interview. These challenges are persistent themes from all the participants:

   a) Concept of Time – How can one share life with a community that has no time for new friends?
   b) Trust – How does one build trust in a community that does not have time?
   c) Relationship – How might one build a relationship when there is no trust?
   d) Community engagement – How does one build a community to an individualistic or independent culture?
   e) Lack of training in apologetics and theology to a highly rational nation.
   f) How can one foster leadership development amidst an "unforgiving society"—a society that exhibits and requires political correctness?
   g) The same evangelism and discipleship principles but different in application.
   h) Need for intercultural communication competency as part of a diverse leadership team.
   i) What are missiological paradigm shifts necessary to lead from monocultural background to intercultural (from Victory to Every Nation)?
   j) How do you contextualize the endless possibilities of contextualization?
   k) What is the Good News for rich people?

Despite these challenges Filipinos face in the global north, one participant said, "at the end of the day, I know I am a child of God."

After synthesizing the participant's answers through concept mapping, I identified their responses following Lewis' Force Field Analysis as either restraining or driving forces. These forces are categorized into a) physical forces (physical abilities like the location of the building, technology), b) psychological forces (attitudes, motivation for change, habit, personal or religious beliefs), and c) group forces (school culture, social attitudes such as stereotypes of groups of people).

The dark green font represents the restraining forces, and the dark red font represents the driving forces to distinguish between the restraining and driving forces. It is noticeable that there are restraining and driving forces in each category.

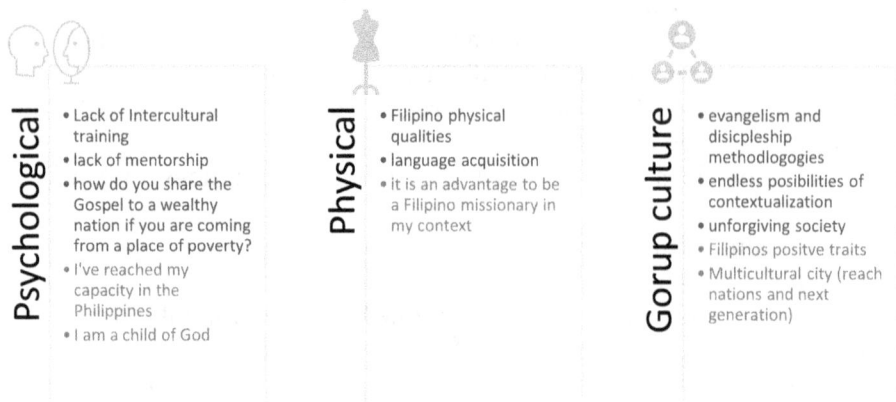

Psychological
- Lack of Intercultural training
- lack of mentorship
- how do you share the Gospel to a wealthy nation if you are coming from a place of poverty?
- I've reached my capacity in the Philippines
- I am a child of God

Physical
- Filipino physical qualities
- language acquisition
- it is an advantage to be a Filipino missionary in my context

Gorup culture
- evangelism and disicpleship methodlogogies
- endless posibilities of contextualization
- unforgiving society
- Fillpinos positve traits
- Multicultural city (reach nations and next generation)

Figure 4 Psychological, Physical, and Group Culture Forces

Psychological

The driving force of reaching their capacity in the Philippines expressed during the interview "there is no more land to conquer" plus their response to God's calling presented new challenges to the Filipino missionaries that are inevitable, the lack of intercultural training, lack of mentorship, and sharing the gospel in their context. Most of their friends in ministry are in the Philippines, and no one can share or empathize with their challenges as first-generation Filipino missionaries in their context.

Physical

While most participants see being a Filipino missionary as an advantage to their local context, their physical look suggests challenges in their context. It ranges from obvious racism to altering the public image or simple name change. However, even though they willingly alter their fashion to reach other nationalities, their identity in Christ still matters at the end of the day. One missionary said it so well, despite other people's opinion and perception of Filipinos: "I know which family I belong to," referring to their place as a co-heir with Christ; a truly kingdom-oriented mission.

Group Culture

One consistent theme throughout the interview is the evangelism and discipleship language and methodologies within the organization. Over decades of being Filipino missionaries in the Philippines, they had already acquired evangelism methodologies and practices. Intercultural conflict is inevitable when joining an established local church in the global north, where many churches have existed twenty years or more. It sparked some

42

misunderstandings regarding the *application* of those principles in their context. There is a gap in understanding why it worked in the Philippines and not in the global north. Added to this dilemma, they moved from a monocultural environment to diverse cities where the necessity of contextualization is endless. However, Filipinos are resilient, trustworthy, generous, adaptable, and patient. These positive traits and the desire to reach the next generation through international students and highly concentrated migrating families in the city are enough for the Filipino missionaries to stay and hopefully inspire more Filipino missionaries to the global north.

Restraining and Driving Forces

This graph shows the merging of the three categories showing the relationship between the restraining force and driving force. A force field analysis identifies forces that push for change and forces that are resisting change. [120] Without action or intervention, this status will remain the same.

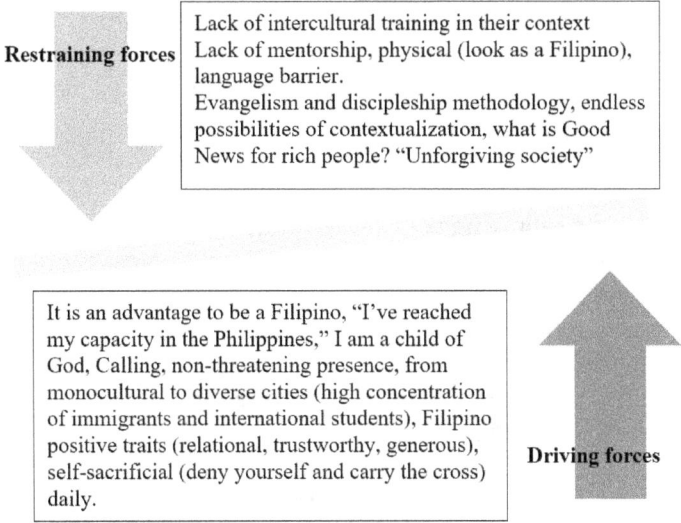

Restraining forces

> Lack of intercultural training in their context
> Lack of mentorship, physical (look as a Filipino), language barrier.
> Evangelism and discipleship methodology, endless possibilities of contextualization, what is Good News for rich people? "Unforgiving society"

> It is an advantage to be a Filipino, "I've reached my capacity in the Philippines," I am a child of God, Calling, non-threatening presence, from monocultural to diverse cities (high concentration of immigrants and international students), Filipino positive traits (relational, trustworthy, generous), self-sacrificial (deny yourself and carry the cross) daily.

Driving forces

Figure 5 Restraining and Driving Forces

According to Lewis' Force Field Theory, the way to disturb the quasi-stationary equilibrium is to decrease the restraining forces and increase the driving forces.

---

[120] Johnson and Christensen, *Educational Research*, 59.

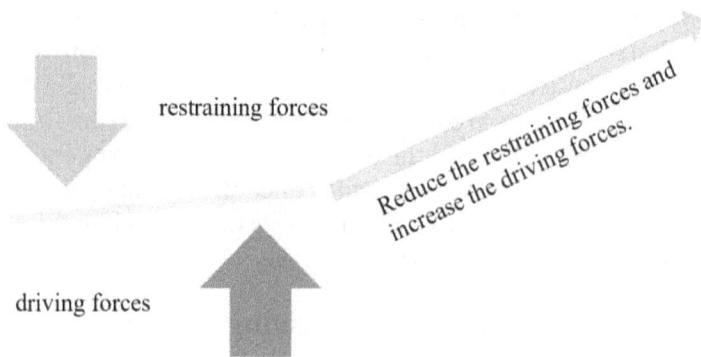

Figure 6 Disequilibrium for Change

Earlier in this chapter, I introduced the first-generation Filipino missionaries who participated in my research. We learned about their ministry background, motivation, and how they became missionaries to the global north. Several themes emerged through the interview process and were classified into three factors: psychological, physical, and group culture. The above graphs showed the coalesce of restraining and driving forces according to Lewis' Force Field Analysis.

I can now make the following conclusive findings based on the inquiry:

a) The restraining and driving forces are constant unless there is an intervention.
b) Intercultural competency training and mentorship will solve most of the gaps in missions.
c) Relationality in Christian practice and missions is a value for first-generation Filipino missionaries.
d) Understanding diaspora missions will increase the participants' involvement in becoming an intercultural church.
e) Ministry to international students and the younger generation is valuable.

Four Challenges and Action Plan

In the previous chapter, I presented the restraining and driving forces Filipino missionaries experience in the global north. Lewis proposed two ways from his Force Field Analysis theory to break the quasi-equilibrium state, 1) decrease the restraining forces and 2) increase the driving forces. This section will discuss how to decrease the restraining forces that Filipino missionaries encounter at the beginning stage of evangelism and discipleship by means of intercultural competency. Four intercultural conflicts emerged based on the interview, context (high or low contexts), time orientation, trust formation, and degree of interdependence (individualistic or collectivist). Some of the questions raised during the interview were:

a) Time – How does one share life with a community that has no time for new friends?
b) Trust – How does one build trust in a community that is time-famished?
c) Relationship – How does one build a relationship when trust is lacking?
d) Community engagement – How does one build a community within an individualistic or independent culture?

High-Context and Low-Context Cultures

"Discipleship is Relationship."

In campus ministry, food plays a significant part in a gathering. Moreover, in my culture and experiences as a campus missionary in the Philippines, I was fully convinced that food draws people towards an event. Oftentimes it is the center of an event. Part of my daily routine was to go to a campus, set up a table with some food or snacks to interview students for the "Spiritual Pulse Survey."[121] The idea is to have students stop for food and have a conversation with me. In my experience with the students of Seattle, the reverse happened. The students of Seattle stopped for the survey more and had far less interest in the food. Even though I would say, "please take some food," they had second thoughts not because they are shy but because they want to know, "Is this apple/banana organic?" or "Sorry, I don't drink soda! It's poison." They looked at the food relatively uninterested and walked away. As more students joined our community group, they asked if I would serve gluten-free or vegan options for our weekly gatherings. Suddenly, my Filipino recipes lacked popularity, and with a sharp look on my face, I responded, "I am not your caterer; if you want other food, bring your own requests." Surprisingly, they did come with their own food.

The city of Seattle is my first long-term cross-cultural mission experience. I had no intercultural competency training before the move. The few times I visited Seattle were mainly to seek God's confirmation for my life and if He was indeed leading me in this new direction after being a campus missionary in the Philippines for almost ten years. The city is known for many things, its environmental advocacies, activism, and clean air. The citizens are health enthusiasts; bikers and runners are a common everyday sight, and they are known to choose healthier options for food like vegan, vegetarian, gluten-free, organic, and so on—a small piece of information I wished I knew then.

---

[121] Spiritual Pulse Survey is a 10-set question survey to engage students in spiritual conversation, developed by Greg Mitchell, an Every Nation pastor in Vancouver, Canada. We experienced some hostile engagements initially when we use "The God Test," a similar tool by Rice Brooks; it is well known within Every Nation Global Family of Churches as the main engagement tool for college campuses to "address skepticism, critical issues of faith and the meaning of life," See www.thegodtest.com.

My story is not unique to the participants of this research. It might be as simple as serving food to as complex as evangelism and discipleship methodologies. As mentioned in the previous chapter, the concept "discipleship is relationship" is a well-known phrase and practice in the Philippines regarding evangelism and discipleship. This concept is lived, witnessed, modeled, and shared within Victory Philippines. When the participants were asked by someone from their context, "what is discipleship?" their immediate response was "discipleship is relationship" or "the Four E's (engage, establish, equip, and empower). If you ask them to itemize it for you, this is where the breakdown happens. For Filipinos and other nationalities who belong to high-context cultures, the knowledge came from lived or shared experiences. The epistemology of "discipleship is relationship" emerged from shared life experiences passed on to them. Before this phrase came to be, it was lived, modeled, heard, talked about, and witnessed for years. It was a cycle, a pattern that eventually became a lifestyle. So, to ask them, "what exactly is discipleship?," the answer was embedded within a ton of references, contextual cues, nuances, and weight of experiences. It is unnecessary, or even impossible, to say it explicitly. Instead, they understand and know *how* to make disciples. When a first-generation Filipino missionary joins a team with a low-context culture, intercultural conflict occurs. Low-context cultures expect explicit, clear, and direct answers. To illustrate this conflict, I will use an iceberg as an illustration. An iceberg has two parts, what is visible, and what is below the ocean. If you are to ask one, "What is an iceberg?" The tendency is to choose one over the other, depending on which reality one lives on. Say on a cruise, a tourist is more concerned with the visible portion of the icebergs for photos, but for seafarers whose living quarters are at the bottom part of the ship, they could hear the icebergs hitting the sides of the ocean liner, the bottom part of the iceberg is much closer to their reality.

In the same way, defining or understanding discipleship for low-context looks at what is seen, explicit, and clear, while high-context cultures rely heavily on shared assumptions and common reference points. The intercultural conflict is that they have a different reality. The top iceberg cannot see what is below and vice versa.

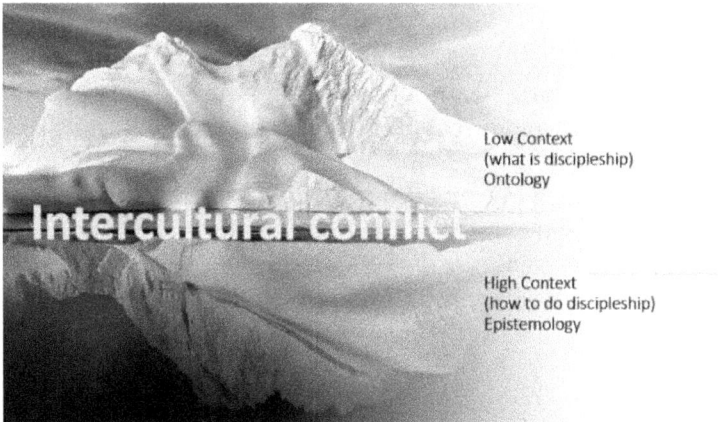

Figure 7 Iceberg Illustration Between High and Low Contexts

Cultures from the global north are consequently low-context cultures. They define discipleship ontologically (what is the reality), while Filipinos understand it from an epistemological perspective (how this knowledge came to be). The reality for the global north is what is seen, "this city is a difficult place to share the Gospel, unlike the Philippines," which is true. Meanwhile, Filipino missionaries reason from, "I have seen this before, thousands were baptized from where I came from, God can do it again," which is also true. The intercultural conflict is from two different philosophies of engagement trying to answer the same question. One answers the question *"what is the reality?"* in our situation, and the other shares from what *"he/she experienced"* in the Philippines. Truth formation is based on reality by the former and through lived experiences by the latter.

Trust and Relationship

Trust or Relationship, Which Comes First.

Trust is a concept that "everybody understands, but few people can accurately define much less measure."[122] Some words associated with trust are integrity, honesty, credibility, or perception. However, during the interview, I noticed how my participants use relationship and trust interchangeably, "we want to build a relationship in our community before we can share the gospel, and in building a relationship we need to build trust," or "for them to trust us, we need to build a relationship with them." It is a both/and concept, a significant Eastern pattern of thinking.[123] Therefore, it is evident to combine the two, trust and relationships, into this section. It is worth mentioning that in

---

[122] "Trust," Communication Research Trends 39, No. 4 (2020): 3. Gale Academic Onefile), Accessed Aprl 28, 2021, https://link.gale.com/apps/doc/a646888170.

[123] edwin Hoffman And Arjan Verdooren, *Diversity Competence: Cultures Don't Meet, People Do* (Boston, Ma: Cabi, 2019), 206.

chapter four, most of my participants became part of the community first before they surrendered their lives to Christ. In that community, they served and witnessed lives transformed. They started attending classes with their friends in that community and strengthened their theology for this newfound faith.

In business settings, Erin Meyer, author of *Culture Map*, pointed out two forms of trust: affective and cognitive. The more a culture tends toward task-based trust, the more they separate affective and cognitive trust, mainly relying on cognitive trust for work relationships. Inversely, the further the culture is towards relationship-based trust the more cognitive and affective trust are forged together.[124]

To understand the concept of trust and relationships between cultures, I will use Erin Meyer's Compare Culture Map tool.[125] The figure below shows where Filipinos posit on the trust scale and the nations from the global north represented in this research. A typical Filipino's culture is the solid black circle, and the contexts represented by the Filipino missionaries are the solid black triangles. Although one is relatively closer, all contexts formed their trust through task-oriented activities.

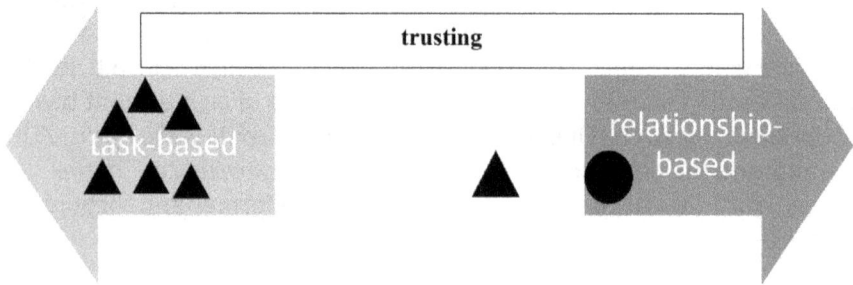

Figure 8 Task-based and Relationship-based

Meyer described the two categories as,

Task-based trust is built through business-related activities. Work relationships are built and dropped easily, based on the practicality of the situation. You do good work consistently, you are reliable. Therefore, 'I enjoy working with you, I trust you.' However, relationship-based trust formation begins in sharing meals, drinks, visits at the coffee machine. Work relationships build slowly over the long term. I've seen who you are at a

---

[124] Erin Meyer, *The Culture Map: Breaking Through the Invisible Boundaries of Global Business* (New York, NY: Public Affairs, 2014) 163-170.
[125] Erin Meyer, "The Country Mapping Tool," accessed April 27, 2021, https://erinmeyer.com/tools/culture-map.

deep level, I've shared personal time with you, I know others who trust you, therefore 'I trust you.'[126]

At the surface level, one can see the disconnection when a Filipino missionary begins to engage a task-based community; there is no shared workspace where Filipinos can prove themselves as trustworthy. First-generation Filipino missionaries must first re-orient their understanding of building trust through task-related activities and then invite them to a more relational connection after, such as dinner or coffee. It would take humility and servanthood to practice this, as the familiar stories of Overseas Filipino Workers mentioned in chapter two. The OFWs gained their employer or co-workers' trust within a work setting (task-based) as nannies, nurses, engineers even in hard places known as the 10/40 window. It enabled them to gain access and build trust. Their hard work and good work ethic gave them the platform to share the gospel. Trust was established first in the work setting. It will take consistency and patience before the right opportunity comes.

In contrast to first-generation Filipino missionaries in the global northencou define their community as the ones who are non-Christians, the lost, the community they need to minister. *Though this is true, they must understand that their first community engagement is the leadership team they are part of.* They must shift their gears that their first opportunity to display exemplary work ethics is their engagement with the leadership team within the institution. Most of the participants in this research are part of an established church and sit on the leadership or strategic meetings. Their primary community is the leadership team. The outreach community is second; both are important. When missionaries choose to focus their attention on sharing the gospel to the lost alone and neglect their relationship with the team, it contravenes Jesus' prayer for the unity among the believers in John chapter seventeen "Then the world will know that you sent me and have loved them even as you have loved me" (John 17: 23, New International Version). The unity displayed by the believers is a testament to the world that the Father loves them.

In the business world, Meyer said that the "center of gravity in the global business world has fundamentally shifted over the past fifteen years," where the United States used to dominate most world markets. Today, the BRIC (Brazil, Russia, India, and China) cultures are on the rise in the global business, all positioned on a relationship-based, trusting scale. To be successful as an international manager in the global market is to excel in a relationship-based trusting scale—this same phenomenon mentioned in chapter one regarding a shift in the centrality of Christianity. Bringing in relationship-based orientation to task-based cultures might take a much longer time and patience to see the response, but it is long-lasting.

As a general rule of thumb, investing time in developing a relationship-based approach will pay dividends when working with people from around the

126 Meyer, *The Culture Map,* 171.

world. This is true even if you both come from task-based cultures, such as the United States and Germany. Once an affective relationship is established, forgiveness for any cultural missteps you make comes a lot easier. So, when you work internationally, no matter who you are working with, investing more time in building trust is a good idea. But knowing exactly how to build affective trust may not always be so obvious. [127]

Concept of Time

Chronos and Kairos

Another complexity added to building relationships is finding the time. Filipino missionaries invite task-based oriented cultures to spend time with them to get to know them, yet there is a disparity between cultures in its value for time.

Hoffman and Verdooren classified chronemics, the study of time and communication, into two, the monochroneous and polychroneous.[128] Monochroneous societies value time as a limited resource. This may be expressed as "time is money" or "time is gold." When frustrated, one would often say, "I just wasted my time." In "Greek, *Chronos* means clock-time, and in pre-Socratic philosophy, *Chronos* is the personification of time, often referred to as the father of time."[129] The father of time is depicted as an old man and with a long white beard. They operate in deadlines, precision, conciseness, and punctuality. Scheduled appointments are preferred rather than spontaneity. They usually suffer from a lack of time, and their pet peeve is waiting. Activities are filtered if it is worth their time or if it is time-consuming.

The second type of time orientation is polychroneous, time that becomes ripe with waiting. In Greek mythology, *Kairos* is the "personification of opportunity, luck, and favorable moments. He is depicted with only one lock of hair, easily seized upon arrival but once passed, no one could grasp him for the back of his head is bald."[130] If the moment has passed, no one can bring back time, so one has also missed the opportunity. Societies in polychroneous time are very adaptable, flexible, and can multitask. Time is fluid, respected, and not something to be disrupted. Waiting for the right time is a value. For them, maintaining good social relations is essential for performing tasks.

---

[127] Meyer, 178.
[128] Hoffman and Verdooren, *Diversity Competence*, 178.
[129] Hoffman and Verdooren, 178.
[130] Hoffman and Verdooren, 178.

Value of time

Monochronic   Polychronic

Figure 9 Monochronic and Polychronic

One participant mentioned that when she asked a local if she would like to get coffee with her, the local immediately pulled out her calendar app on her phone and replied, "When, where, and what time?" The Filipino missionary found herself searching for an immediate time and place, but she took that incident as a lesson: when you invite someone from a monochroneous society, you should be ready with the details.

When I was a student at the School of World Missions in the Philippines, sixteen out of forty of the students came from different nations. I asked one of my classmates if she would like to hang out with me after class and grab a coffee. She looked at me quizzically and asked, "Why?" Thankfully, we just returned from an out-of-town outreach activity the past weekend, and I replied, "I want to show some of the pictures we have from our outreach." She agreed to go with me, and we had a great time. Coffee after school became our habit, and she became one of my closest friends in the school. On our graduation day, she handed me a small gift. It was a handful of our pictures together during school and a card. The note on the card said, "Thank you for inviting me for coffee after class even though I first asked you, 'Why?' – your Singaporean friend." Consequently, high-context cultures operate in polychroneous time orientation, and low-context cultures are monochronic.

Table 4 Monochronic and Polychronic Time Orientations

Monochroneous	Polychroneous
Father of time= clock time	Personification of opportunity, luck, and favorable moments,
- "time is gold" "time is money."	- time is respected and not to be disrupted
-	- time is fluid
operate in deadlines, punctuality, and precision	
- "I do not want to waste time."	- they are adaptable and flexible
- filter activities if it is worth their time or time-consuming	- good social relations is vital in performing tasks
- waiting is a pet peeve	- time becomes ripe with waiting
Countries from:	Countries from:
Low-context cultures	High-context cultures

Filipinos operate in polychroneous times. Based on the challenges discussed in chapter four, Filipino missionaries and locals value time differently. Filipinos have expressed their challenges in the early stage of evangelism, asking, "Where do you find time to build relationships?" Unfortunately, this is also a challenge among international students in the global north. The need to study and work simultaneously is often expected, unlike in the Philippines, where their parents or extended families financially support most college students. This value for education is common among Filipinos. Parents want their children to excel in school and eventually help the family move out of poverty. Therefore, they will do everything to make education their only burden.

Dawna Ballard, a professor at the University of Texas and scholar of chronemics, said, "Time is really at the heart of our quality of life."[131] Furthermore, she mentioned Edward Hall (1914-2009), a well-known anthropologist and cross-cultural researcher, who asserts that, "Time is an invisible language. We send messages through time constantly, and we assume life will unfold according to a certain tempo, he observed, but that language and those assumptions change across cultures."[132] Since the industrial revolution, time and punctuality, according to Ballard, became an adversarial and disciplining force, in that how you handle time is a measurement of virtue as a person.[133] When Filipinos value time differently from monochronic cultures, a potential intercultural conflict awaits. The hosting culture might perceive them

---

[131] "Reclaiming My Time': Strategies From A Scholar Of Chronemics, The Study Of Time." Quartz, August 5, 2017. Gale Academic Onefile, Accessed April 28, 2021, Https://Link.Gale.Com/Apps/Doc/ A499919263.

[132] "Reclaiming My Time."

[133] "Reclaiming My Time."

initially as lazy. As simple as setting an appointment to "hang out" or "spend time" is already a challenge.

However, Ballard also pointed out that the clock is an organizing and coordinating tool to *foster human relationships* to achieve something together. Allow me to highlight one of Ballard's points in her article "Reclaiming Time":

> When we falsely see time as this external entity (or what the Greeks called *Chronos*), rather than something we create (*Kairos*), the fear of not being punctual can easily put us into fight or flight mode, sweating and becoming nauseated, or aggressive when we're late for work or behind on a project. It's not the wild animal that's chasing us now, as it did our earliest ancestors, says Ballard. It's the unforgiving clock. Just becoming aware that this ferocious beast is our own creation can be liberating.[134]

Low context cultures consequently value time in monochronic ways. They filter activities based on their assessment of time, and time is gold. Therefore, they usually operate in high efficiency with the shortest possible amount of time. It may affect their approach to evangelism and discipleship because, in reality, forming relationships takes time, and the reward for following Christ is not always measurable from an earthly perspective.

Individualism and Collectivism

How do you Engage an Individualistic Community?

Individualistic mindset might reason that, "I do not have to build new friendships; I already have my family and the government who will take care of my needs." How then, do you build community in individualistic societies?

Hoffman and Verdooren listed six orientations on how people engage with one another.[135] In this section, I will only focus on how individualism and collectivism influence people's interactions. This cultural orientation determines the "degree of interdependence a society maintains among its members."[136]

Cultures with a collectivist orientation are strongly connected to others, dependent on one another, and loyal to their community.[137] It influences their decisions by what is better for the group rather than for the individual. Their focuses are in-group goals, the context more than the content in

---

[134] "Reclaiming my Time."

[135] The six orientations are collectivism vs individualistic, masculine vs feminine, division and of roles between men and women, hierarchical vs egalitarian, universal and particularistic, and specific vs diffuse. Hoffman and Verdooren, *Diversity Competency*, 220.

[136] "Country Comparison," Hofstede's Insights, accessed April 29, 2021, https://www.hofstede-insights.com/country-comparison.

[137] Hoffman and Verdooren, *Diversity Competence*, 221.

communication, and defining relationships as communal.[138] Their self-image is defined by "we" and "they take care of each other in exchange for loyalty."[139] For instance, a Filipino high school graduate decides what program to take in college, depending on what the parents suggest or decide and beneficial for the whole family. One would often ask oneself, "If I pursue this career, will it alleviate my family from poverty or bring honor to the family?" Such a practice is common among Filipinos and Asian families. Another specific example mentioned from the interview was when they decided whether they should go to full-time ministry. Many of them first considered how it would affect their family financially and relationally.

Individualistic-oriented cultures are motivated by personal concerns, freedom, and satisfaction.[140] They believe that as long as one is able to make decisions, they should be left to take care of themselves. One of the participants validated this observation as one of the shocking revelations she encountered in her context. She said, "Even though the person's life is at risk, as long as the person is capable of making a decision, no one should intervene."[141]

Individualistic   Collectivist

personal concern and freedom	strongly connected to others
self-image is defined by "I"	self-image is defined by "we"
look after themselves and their direct families	motivated by what is good for the ingroup members (family, extended family or kinsmen)

Figure 10 Individualistic and Collectivist Cultures

An intercultural conflict occurs when collectivist cultures see individualistic cultures as soloists while individualistic cultures may see the collectivist as a dependent. One participant expressed concerns about being willing to learn in her new context, "But no one was willing to show [her] how."[142]

---

[138] Harry C. Triandis and H C Triandis, "Individualism-Collectivism and Personality," *Journal of Personality* 69, no. 6 (December 2001): 907–924, accessed April 29, 2021, http://search.ebscohost.com.

[139] "Country Comparison," Hofstede's Insights, accessed April 29, 2021, https://www.hofstede-insights.com/country-comparison.

[140] Hoffman and Verdooren, *Diversity Competence*, 221.

[141] "All interviews are confidential; the names of the interviewees are withheld by mutual agreement." Interviewed by Ria L. Martin. Seattle. March 31, 2021.

[142] "All interviews are confidential; the names of the interviewees are withheld by mutual agreement." Interviewed by Ria L. Martin. Seattle. April 2, 2021.

These two opposing orientations birthed the need for mentorship. The participants have expressed that having a mentor on the field would help bridge the gap. Mentorship may be unnecessary for an individualistic culture, but for first-generation Filipino missionaries, who are treading new territories, this is vital in their support system and success as relational communities. Many emphasized in the interview that, "I need someone whom I can bounce back my ideas with, as well as give me feedback."

Section Summary

At the beginning of this chapter, I propounded Lewis's theory to decrease the restraining forces through intercultural competency as one of the two ways to disturb the quasi-equilibrium state. The themes from the interview resulted in a lack of intercultural competency training and mentorship. I embarked on each component based on the emerging themes from chapter four. These are contexts (high and low contexts), trust formation, time orientation, and degree of interdependence (individualistic or collectivist culture). Through the above discussion and illustrations, I have presented where Filipinos stand in relation to their new cultural contexts in the global north. The participants in my research are first-generation Filipino missionaries to the global north. Decreasing the restraining forces through self-awareness is the first step to intercultural competency.

Proposed Action Plan

Imago Dei

In chapter two, I mentioned the works of Pantoja, Luis, Sadiri Joy Tira, and Enoch Wan in the book *Scattered: The Filipino Global Presence* regarding Filipinos massive migration that began in the 1970s. The OFWs (overseas Filipino workers) sought opportunities abroad by working as seafarers, nannies, nurses, and engineers and how the forced migration led to the propagation of the Christian faith. Filipino diasporas' adaptability enabled them to contextualize churches creatively in buses, ocean liners, and hospitals. Tira and Stuart Lightbody, the First Filipino Alliance Church (FFAC) in Edmonton, Alberta, documented the cyclical and glocal nature of the Filipino International Network that gave birth to the first Filipino Alliance Church, reaching the nations through Filipinos. Tira's ethnographic research on *Filipino Kingdom Workers* provides testimonials of Filipino diasporas, the OFWs, taking the gospel to other nations, such as Europe and Hong Kong. He claimed that this strategy is the most cost-effective mission strategy, compared to direct support sent to missionaries. That direct-support approach has been the norm for decades, but limits mission sending to only wealthy nations. These research studies and statistics are pieces of evidence that Filipino diasporas thrive in other nations, professionally and missionally. Their exposure to hardships and natural disasters developed their adaptability, resilience, and creativity when faced with opposition and challenges, making them successful as ministers of the gospel, especially in creative access nations.

In addition to this, Sonia Zaide, author of *The Philippines: A Unique Nation*, argues that the Philippines is a unique nation "due to its heritage from four major civilizations—the Asian, the European, the Latin, and the American."[143]

This chapter will not make any attempt at solving marginalization, systemic racism, or institutionalized segregation. Gorospe mentioned how Filipinos experience marginalization in two ways, socially and structurally invisible and subaltern experiences. The author does not deny its existence either. Rather, the participants verified Gorospe's findings as Filipinos continue to experience marginalization in the global north.

This section *does* hope to elucidate a more personal question regarding how a Filipino diaspora should respond to missions when there *is* marginalization or increase their driving force in missions through the concept of *Kapwa*.

Donald Smith, the author of *Creating Understanding,* writes, "Communication is a process for creating understanding in which two or more parties are involved."[144] There are two relational foci for this section: 1) the relationship between God and a Filipino diaspora (vertically) and 2) the relationship between a Filipino diaspora and the community he/she serves (horizontally).

The Relationship Between God and a Filipino Diaspora as Imago Dei

The first order in understanding our relationship with others is to understand the relationships at work within the Trinity. We look at the trinitarian relationships to model or pattern after our relationships with others. In chapter two, I cited Leithart's explanations of Trinitarian relationships, both immanent and economic. To summarize again: immanent refers to the intra-trinitarian relationship that is exclusive and eternal; economic refers to the Trinitarian relationships revealed within the history of Jesus Christ. To echo Leithart, Horrell, Wan, and Hedinger, the economic Trinity is an accurate representation, but it is not the complete and totality of God. Leithart explains the doctrine of the Trinity as a practical doctrine.

> It tells us what God is like, it tells us what we are to be like, it says something about the kind of God that we worship and the way God interacts with us and with the world. As we understand more and more what the Bible reveals to us about the Father, Son, and Holy Spirit, the more practical the doctrine becomes (Leithart, 2016).

Genesis one is fundamental to our identity and calling. When God said, "So God created mankind in his own image, in the image of God he created them;

---

[143] Sonia M. Zaide, *The Philippines: A Unique Nation* (All-Nations Publishing, 1999), cover page.
[144] Donald K. Smith, *Creating Understanding: Christian Communication Across Cultural Landscapes*, 1 edition. (Books On Creating Understanding, 2014), cover page.

male and female he created them" (Gen. 1:27, New English Translation), He established who we are (identity) and what we are called to do (calling/purpose) in the context of community. As created in God's image, our identity and purpose are interconnected; both are timeless and encompassing. It transcends peoples of every nation, tribe, and language throughout time because it is an extension of His character as our Triune God. However, in Genesis 3, the direct access was broken when "they hid from the LORD in the garden" (Gen 3:8, New English Translation). When humanity's identity and calling to reflect God's image was exchanged to self-definition of identity and calling, Jesus came and restored that. The Letter to the Hebrews testifies,

> After God spoke long ago in various portions and in various ways to our ancestors through the prophets, in these last days, he has spoken to us in a son, whom he appointed heir of all things, and through whom he created the world. The Son is the radiance of his glory and the representation of his essence, and he sustains all things by his powerful word, and so when he had accomplished cleansing for sins, he sat down at the right hand of the Majesty on high. Thus he became so far better than the angels as he has inherited a name superior to theirs. (Heb 1:1-4, New English Translation).

Jesus Christ is the radiance of God's glory and representation of his essence; his crucifixion and resurrection restored humanity's calling and identity. The Gospel of Matthew asserts that he restored all authority in heaven and on earth and has given his disciples an extension of that restored authority to make disciples of all nations (Matt 28:18-20). Humanity's calling and identity in His image is possible through His Son Jesus Christ by the power of the Holy Spirit. Jesus made it possible for us, as Paul addressed the church in Philippi, to be united in Christ and to have the same mindset as Christ Jesus.

This section has established that humanity's timeless identity and calling is to reflect God's character as his image. Thus, it is first fundamental for a Filipino diaspora to understand that his/her identity and calling, as God's image-bearers, are interconnected. Secondly, it is essential to see oneself and others as created in the image of God. This is how God sees him/her, and this is how one should view others.

The second relational focus is the horizontal relationship between a Filipino diaspora and his/her community.

Filipino Diaspora Towards Others

Above, I noted that Gorospe mentions the marginalization experienced by Filipino diasporas who, despite their successful missional stories, continue to experience this marginalization in their local context.

First, I offer an anecdote: there is a Filipino community center in South Seattle. As soon as I walk into this center, it feels like walking in one of the buildings in the Philippines back home; the flowers, portraits of Saints, the small food station with Filipino *merienda,* and the Filipino soap operas playing on television. Although it fosters familiarity and a small taste of home, consequently, it also fosters "Otherness" in the minds of both the migrant and host. Paul Woods wrote that "acknowledging someone is different from ourselves is not inherently wrong or harmful; indeed it is part of our self-definition."[145] This is indeed correct. We all have a different perception of otherness to the people we meet. Woods quotes Zizoulas regarding the problem of the "other" in the locus of Western Culture:

> In our culture, protection from the other is a fundamental necessity. We feel more and more threatened by the presence of the other. We are forced and even encouraged to consider the other as our enemy before we can treat him or her as our friend. Communion with the other is not spontaneous; it is built upon fences which protect us from the dangers implicit in the other's presence. We accept the other only in so far as he or she does not threaten our privacy or in so far as he or she is useful for our individual happiness.[146]

When a Filipino or a minority congregate (intentionally or unintentionally) with her/his kinsmen, it forms a stronger presence in the community. What seems harmless (preservation of the community, strong connection to kinsmen, loyalty to one's own people) is perceived initially as a threat or as an enemy—this is the first challenge Filipino diasporas need to understand and overcome in missions. Before a minority can be considered a friend, he/she is first a threat. Woods adds, "Otherness between host and migrant, on individual and group basis, is an essential element in missional encounters between Christian communities and incoming migrants."[147] What often happens is that a cultural pattern is formed wherein a minority group gathers, and in response, the perception of them as a threat is heightened. When a threat or exclusion is felt more than an acceptance or embracing of the minority group, that minority group will strengthen their bond, look for other minority groups and expand their presence, magnifying the already existing threat perceived by the host community. This pattern feeds fear and insecurity in a cyclical way emerging from both migrants and hosts. Today, we see societies with pockets of minority groups on one end and locals on another end. Even though both may have good intentions of breaking the cycle, this cultural force contributes to marginalization

---

[145] Paul Woods in "God, Israel, The Church and the Other: Otherness, as a Theological Motif in Diaspora Mission" in *Scattered and Gathered: A Global Compendium of Diaspora Missiology* (Oxford, England: Regnum Books International, 2016), 135.

[146] Woods, 135.

[147] Woods, 134.

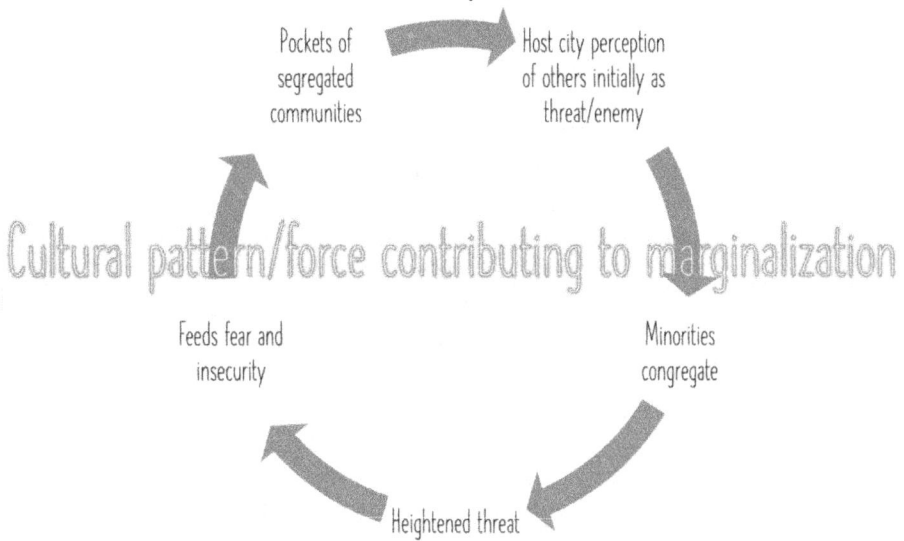

Cultural pattern/force contributing to marginalization

Pockets of segregated communities → Host city perception of others initially as threat/enemy → Minorities congregate → Heightened threat → Feeds fear and insecurity →

Figure 11 Cultural Pattern of Marginalization

Woods again quotes Zizioulas, who introduced St. Maximus' Difference and Division in chapter seven of the book *Scattered and Gathered,* that

> Difference is the healthy acknowledgment, positive and accepting of Otherness; while Division is the negative, discriminating, and toxic response to Otherness. When we come across a migrant or outsider to our community, what can be done to go beyond seeing him or her simply as a representative of a larger group? How much of our fear of the Other is actually a reflection of our own inadequacy and insecurity? How can our identity in Christ remove the need for self-affirmation, which is often sought by denigrating the Other?[148] (Woods 2016, 145)

In this story, sadly, division wins.

Kapwa a Scriptural Approach to Marginalization in Missions

One of the first few ways to engage in cross-cultural missions as a diaspora is to strive to know and understand your context. Putting together the right modules and training will contribute to the success of the missionary's work. While this part of the training is essential, let us not forget that "immigrants too contribute to the culture of the city as they are shaped by it." [149] For instance, when migrants move to a new place, they bring their religious beliefs and

---

[148] Woods, 145.

[149] Enoch Wan and Anthony Casey, *Church Planting among Immigrants in US Urban Centers (Second Edition): The "Where", "Why", And "How" of Diaspora,* 2 edition. (Portland, OR: CreateSpace Independent Publishing Platform, 2016), 62.

traditions with them. When I moved to Seattle in 2012, I was surprised to see an amulet, a small picture of a saint that my mom secretly tucked in my luggage as a sign of protection. One international student in our campus ministry told me that she has been wearing a buddha necklace her mom gave her since she was three. More obvious examples are the Buddhism or Hinduism elements, display of patron saints, beads, amulets, or smell of incense in Asian markets or restaurants. Immigrants, Christian or not, contribute to the reshaping of the culture of their host city.

The word "communication" comes from the Latin word *communist,* which means "common."[150] It is finding common ground for understanding in its application. Finding commonality in missions is often sidelined. The default among interculturalists is to show the difference, whether in contrasts or in relation to, between cultures or countries. Hofstede's "Compare Country" tool and Erin Meyer's "Culture Map" are examples of such. Strategies for crossing the boundaries are based on the healthy differences between or among other nationalities. This has been a long-term practice for cross-cultural missionary training for decades. Unfortunately, the foundation of such approaches are difference: what separates *us* from *them*?

Here, I introduce an opposite strategy. It begins with finding commonalities or common ground to understand each other. For Filipinos, the Tagalog term for others is "*kapwa.*" In English translation, it could refer to "neighbors" or what most search engines would suggest: "both." The more appropriate translation of *kapwa,* according to Virgilio Enriquez, the father of Filipino psychology, defines it as the "extension of self in others." The word evokes a sense of dignity, equal space, shared life, shared identity, and deep humanizing value.[151] It communicates what is common or shared—regardless of the differences in culture, economic status, gender, or political affiliations.

Above, I established that humanity's identity and purpose is to reflect God's image. Self-image translates to one's behavior. If a Filipino diaspora sees themselves first as a minority, it will contribute to the cycle of insecurity and fear. To see oneself as created in God's image and extending that self to others is a *sine qua non* in having a Scriptural understanding and approach to missions.

To see others as created in the image of God is consistent with who we are and what we are called to do. Wright helps to define this divine image in his *The Mission of God*:

The expression "in our image" is adverbial (that is, it describes the way God made us), not adjectival (that is as if it simply described a quality we possess). Being created in the image of God is not so much something we possess as what we are. To be human is to be the image of God. It is not an

150 C.S. Rayudu, "Communication," (Mumbai, INDIA: Global Media, 2009), 13, accessed March 2, 2021, http://ebookcentral.proquest.com/lib/westernseminary-ebooks.

151 Jay Yacat, "Filipino Psychology," The Encyclopedia of Cross-Cultural Psychology, Research Gate, accessed December 17, 2021, https://www.researchgate.net/publication.

extra feature added to our species; it is definitive of what it means to be human.[152]

Furthermore, interculturalists Edwin Hoffman and Arjan Verdooren, in their book *Diversity Competence*, propose that,

> Every communication has a content and a relational aspect such that the latter classifies the former, and all communication interchanges are either symmetrical, equal, or complementary (leading-following) depending on whether they are based on equality or difference. [153]

Kapwa and Relational Realism.

Expounding upon the word *kapwa* from the relational realism paradigm helps us understand the relational aspect of missions. In De Leon's presentation of "What Make Filipinos, Filipino?,"[154] he singled out *kapwa* as a Filipino core value and other value-orientations: "that Filipinos love to connect; that Filipinos like to experience the multi-dimensional wholeness of life; and that Filipinos are highly participatory. These characteristics are also evident in Filipino visual art, sculpture, music, architecture, furniture, fashion, and food."[155]

Enriquez said the word is "enwrapped with a *sense of dignity, equal space, shared life, shared identity, and deep humanness value*" (emphasis mine). He further expounds upon in his *kapwa* theory:

> ... a person starts having *kapwa* not so much because of the recognition of status given to him by others but more because of his awareness of shared identity. The *ako* (ego) and the *iba-sa-akin* (others) are one and the same in *kapwa* psychology: *Hindi ako iba sa aking kapwa* (I am no different from others). *Pakikipagkapwa* means accepting and dealing with the other person as an equal.[156]

The relational aspects of *kapwa* in connection to trinitarian relationships explained by Enoch Wan and Mark Hedinger are:[157]

a) Equal space (*perichoresis*: the mutual indwelling of the members of the Trinity)

---

[152] Wright, 421.

[153] Hoffman and Verdooren, 214.

[154] Felipe M. De Leon is the Chairman of National Commission on the Culture and the Arts, professor of Arts Studies, distinguished lecturer and researcher.

[155] Felipe M. De Leon presentation to Athens, Greece on "What makes Filipino, Filipino? Accessed November 4, 2021, https://athenspe.dfa.gov.ph/newsroom/community-news.

[156] Jay Yacat, "Filipino Psychology," The Encyclopedia of Cross-Cultural Psychology, Research Gate, accessed December 17, 2021, https://www.researchgate.net/publication. For additional insights on *Kapwa*, see "Kapwa | Kapwa is Self in Other, Pakikipagkapwa is Sacred Interconnection, (The Principle of Filipino Relationality," <http://pakikipagkapwa.org/.

[157] Wan and Hedinger, *Relational Missionary Training*, 56–57.

b) Shared life (*taxis*: equality of position with diversity in roles and authority)

c) Shared identity (*polyphony*: focus of one member of the Trinity does not diminish the identity of others)

These Trinitarian theological principles model how we should approach horizontal relationships. We all have a different perception of "the other" in the people we meet, and Filipino diasporas are no exception. Smith explains:

> A fuller understanding of communication comes through relationships. Your opinion of your audience will influence what and how you speak to that group. If you feel positive toward your message, your message also tends to be positive. If you expect your audience to be hostile, you will tend to be defensive.[158]

With these explanations in mind, I propose that the Filipino term *kapwa* for others was preserved and embedded in our culture as God's very own idea for relationalism. It is aligned with His attributes, and therefore a Scriptural basis for our approach to missions. In other words, for those who see us as a threat, *kapwa* sees them as created in the image of God, equal in dignity and intrinsic human value.

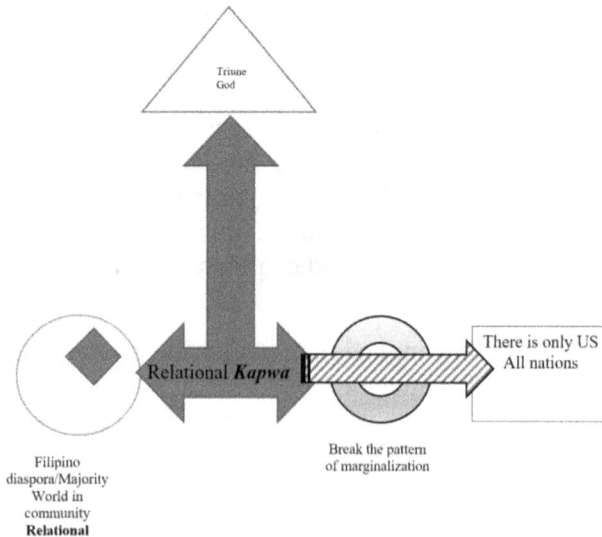

Figure 12 Relational *Kapwa*

Who is Our Own?

> On one occasion, an expert of the law asked Jesus, "Teacher, what must I do to inherit eternal life?" To which Jesus replied, "What is written in the law? How do you understand it?" The expert answered, "Love the LORD your God

---

158 Smith, 177.

with all your heart and with all your soul and with all your strength and with all your mind; and 'Love your neighbor as yourself'" (Luke 10: 25-27, New International Version).

Jesus responses to the expert positively: "You have answered correctly; do this, and you will live." But wanting to justify himself, the man then asked another question, "And who is my neighbor?" Jesus replied with the now well-known parable of the Good Samaritan. In the story, a man was robbed, beaten up, and left half dead. The first two who saw the man on the road were experts of the law, a priest and a Levite; both saw the man and yet turned around. The third person who saw the man on the road was a Samaritan. He took pity on the man and put a bandage on his wound. He did not leave the man on the road; he took him to an inn and paid for the expenses until he was fully recovered. Jesus then asked who of the three acted like a neighbor to the beaten man? The expert of the law said, "the one who showed mercy to him." Jesus said, "Go and do the same" (Luke 10:37, New English Translation).

Excursus

Who are the Samaritans? In the beginning, God chose a couple Sarai and Abraham, to go to the land God called them to go and be a blessing to all nations. They grew into a community and formed the twelve tribes of Israel. They became a united people group under the kingship of Saul, David, and Solomon. But after Solomon's death, the kingdom was fought over by two of his descendants, which caused the estrangement between the Northern Kingdom of Israel and the Southern Kingdom of Judah. Both ended up dramatically destroyed by the Babylonian and Assyrian empires. However, the Bible follows the narrative of the Southern Kingdom more closely, which was exiled and returned to the land after the fall of Babylon to rebuild the Second Temple (see Ezra-Nehemiah). These returnees are those who became the Judeans/Jews.

The Northern Kingdom and its capital Samaria experienced a different kind of exile. The Assyrians, the conquering empire, deported the people repopulated the region with peoples from around the Near East. It destroyed their group identity. What is unique about their exile, in comparison with that of Judah, is that they never returned home and remained scattered. The text from 2 Kings confirms,

The king of Assyria brought people from Babylon, Kuthah, Avva, Hamath and Sepharvaim and settled them in the towns of Samaria to replace the Israelites. They took over Samaria and lived in its towns. When they first lived there, they did not worship the LORD; so he sent lions among them and they killed some of the people. It was reported to the king of Assyria: "The people you deported and resettled in the towns of Samaria do not know what the god of that country requires. He has sent lions among them, which are killing them off, because the people do not know what he requires."

Then the king of Assyria gave this order: "Have one of the priests you took captive from Samaria go back to live there and teach the people what the god of the land requires." So one of the priests who had been exiled from Samaria came to live in Bethel and taught them how to worship the LORD. (2 Kings 17:24-28).

The first mention of the Samaritans is in the book of Nehemiah during the rulership of Persia. "Ezra and the Elephantine papyri reveal a schism between the Jews and the Samaritans during the rebuilding of Jerusalem after the Babylonian captivity" (Maiers, 2016). Ezra 4 testifies to this growing hostility between the two groups. Despite the intention to help, "Let us help you build because, like you, we seek your God and have been sacrificing to him since the time of Esarhaddon king of Assyria, who brought us here," (Ezra 4:2, New International Version), the returnees answered, "you have no part in us with building the temple of our God" (Ezra 4:3, New International Version).

The denouement of this excursus is that for Jews, the Samaritans are the irreconcilably "other" who has no place in worshipping God because their cultural identity is now a mixed people group brought about by the harsh realities of their conquerors. The biblical authors commonly refer to them as pagans and, in the eyes of the Jews, not true worshippers of God. And yet *this* is the people group Jesus chooses to clarify who the expert's neighbor is.

The focus of this story is the answer to the question, "who is my neighbor?" Is a neighbor someone who lives close by? Someone who looks like me? Shares a religious background with me? A "neighbor" is a division mindset that can be traced back to Genesis 4 when Cain responded to God, "Am I my brother's keeper?" This division grew from brother against brother, race against race, men against women, nation against nation, rich against poor, minority against the majority, us against them, and the list go on. The continuing division seemingly makes it harder to grasp, who is one of us? Returning to our gospel story, Jesus picked a Samaritan who is not an expert of the law and yet behaves according to the law by showing mercy to the beaten man. In other words, there are no boundaries in showing mercy. On this concept of "otherness," Paul Hiebert profoundly states that "Scripture leads us to a startling conclusion: at the deepest level of our identity as humans there are *no others—there is only us.*"[159] Sin is what divides us, and that is the division—otherness that we see in them, and they see in us. Hiebert presents human exegesis as one way to bridge the cultural gap between the missionary and the people they serve.[160] Ethnocentrism is a way to exegete one's own. Frequently, ethnocentrism is labeled negatively, but for Filipino diasporas, the term *kapwa,* their own cultural lens to view others, provides leverage in their approach to missions. This approach is discovering the message of the gospel, as God reveals, that are

---

[159] Paul G. Hiebert, *The Gospel in Human Contexts: Anthropological Explorations for Contemporary Missions*, Illustrated edition. (Grand Rapids, Mich: Baker Academic, 2009), 190.
[160] Hiebert, *The Gospel in Human Contexts,* 12.

preserved in our cultures (in this case, through language). For Filipinos and oral learners, these are oral traditions, rituals, images, metaphors, and parables used by the Biblical authors that are hidden riches as God's many ways of communicating to man. Don Richardson referred to such instances as "redemptive analogies"[161] like the story of Peace Child he lived to tell. Richardson says,

> I suggest that just as God has uniquely prepared every people to RECEIVE the Gospel – God has also prepared every people to TAKE the Gospel. All the dynamics, the structures, the systems that are already in every culture, so that when these are redeemed, they enable each culture to make their own unique contribution to global missions.[162]

Smith argues that the cultural patterns of society are fundamentally influenced by its form of communication. Each culture has unique opportunities for the presentation of the gospel of Christ, and effective communication seeks out not just overcoming the differences but finding commonalities as well.

Above, I discussed where Filipinos are positioned in relation to global missions. Even though Filipino diasporas are successful missionally, marginalization is a reality. With Jenkins' projection of the Philippines becoming the third or fourth-largest Christian community on the planet by 2050[163] and the "reverse mission"[164] that is irreversible in the future, missionary opportunities for Filipinos and the Majority World will be broader. As we take the gospel with us, especially among wealthy nations, we will face the reality of marginalization. How we plan and strategize our engagement with the mission communicates volumes about how we understand God's mission and the message of the gospel.

In Romans, Paul states that, "Christ died for the ungodly...while we were still sinners...while we were God's enemies...we were reconciled with him through the death of his son" (Rom 5:6-11, New International Version). Miroslav Volf discussed Christian love as a natural consequence of God's self-giving nature in his book, *Exclusion and Embrace,*

> A genuinely Christian reflection on social issues must be rooted in the self-giving love of the divine Trinity as manifested on the cross of Christ; all central themes of such reflection will have to be thought through from the perspective of the self-giving love of God[165] (Volf, 2019).

---

[161] Michael Pocock and Enoch Wan, eds., *Diaspora Missiology: Reflections on Reaching the Scattered Peoples of the World* (William Carey Library, 2015), kindle loc 881.

[162] Richardson, Don. Peace Child: An Unforgettable Story of Primitive Jungle Treachery in the 20th Century. Gospel Light Publications, 2005.

[163] Jenkins, 1.

[164] Adogame, et al, 1.

[165] Miroslav Volf, *Exclusion and Embrace, Revised and Updated: A Theological Exploration of Identity, Otherness, and Reconciliation*, Revised, Updated edition. (Nashville, TN: Abingdon Press, 2019), 15.

The hunger to see and witness a society that is genuinely united and diverse is becoming more evident. We are indeed in an unprecedented time in Christian history where we are being ushered into modeling a church that Paul addressed in Ephesians. He says that we,

> ...who used to be far away, have been brought near by the blood of Christ. Jesus Christ is our peace, the one who made both groups into one, destroyed the middle wall of partition, the hostility...His purpose is to create in himself one new man (humanity) out of two...he came and preached peace to you...Consequently, you are no longer foreigners and noncitizens, but fellow citizens with saints and members of his household (Ephesians 2:13-22, New English Translation).

In Christ, we can take the gospel of peace even to communities where we are initially perceived as enemies.

Volf noted the Christological and trinitarian themes with Moltmann's *The Spirit of Life,* which he claimes to be the most significant contribution on the implication of the cross for the life in the world.[166] Motlmann's statement bears repeating as a conclusion to this chapter:

> On the cross of Christ this love [i.e., the love of God] is there for the others, for sinners—the recalcitrant—enemies. The reciprocal self-surrender to one another within the Trinity is manifested in Christ's self-surrender in a world which is in contradiction to God; and this self-giving draws all those who believe in him into the eternal life of the divine love.[167]

Relational Christianity and Practices

After discovering the intercultural challenges missionaries face in the global North, the best place to start is for the Filipinos to embrace their aptness as highly relational cultures and this section it will explain why.

Task-oriented cultures approach evangelism and discipleship differently. They embark on business-related activities and practicality. Meyer describes their approach to be short-term. Samuel Escobar coined this term as "managerial missiology"[168] and understands the gospel as a product to be marketed to the target group with measurable goals (i.e., how many people are saved, how many people are baptized, how many came to the outreach event) through carefully crafted strategy. Managerial Missiology is defined by the *Missions Dictionary* as,

> The belief that missions can be approached like a business problem. With the right inputs, the thinking goes, the right outcomes can be assured. Any number of approaches have been hailed as the "key" to world evangelization

---

[166] Volf, 12.
[167] Volf, 13.
[168] Wan, *Diaspora Missiology*, 112.

or to reaching particular groups- everything from contextualization to saturation evangelization.[169]

Through this lens, Christian mission is reduceable to a manageable enterprise. James Engel was one of the proponents of managerial missiology. "He published and co-authored many books in the areas of communication theory, consumer behavior, promotional strategy, proposed the 'Engel Scale' and led missiology in a 'major leap onto the secular stage of strategic planning (David Nett 1999)."[170] Furthermore, Wan critiques Managerial Missiology Paradigm (MMP) as a pragmatic mindset that leads to

> targeting measurable success and quantifiable outcomes. This pragmatic orientation is in line with the research findings of Barna Group in 2010- one of the "six mega-themes" of American Christianity is "growing numbers of people are less interested in spiritual disciples and more desirous of learning pragmatic solutions for life" and at the same time, the Christian Church is becoming less theologically literate (i.e., another theme of the six).[171]

In his book, *Engaging the Secular World through Life-on-Life Discipleship in the British Context,* Wan and Mikeska observed something similar:

> In the UK, there are two main tools in the church used to try to evangelize people: Alpha and Christianity Explored. Both Alpha and Christianity Explored are courses often taught in churches for people interested in learning more about Christianity and Jesus. These courses or programs allow people to explore, think, learn, and ask questions about Christianity and Jesus. While I am not particularly for or against these programs as a basis for enabling people to learn about Christianity and Jesus, I still believe the focus must be on relational disciple-making and not a course. Programs do work and people are being saved and discipled through them. My hope is that we as Christians also model and live out the gospel with people around us.[172]

We learned that Filipinos are culturally relational in their context (high context), trust formation (relationship or affective-based), time orientation (polychroneous), and degree of interdependence (collectivist). Intercultural competency exposed the cultural driving forces between cultures as well as the gaps.

---

[169] Wan, *Diaspora Missiology*, 112

[170] Wan, *Diaspora Missiology*, 114.

[171] Wan, *Diaspora Missiology*, 114.

[172] Wan and Mikeska, *Engaging the Secular World through Life-on-Life Disciple-Making in the British Contex*, 69.

Relational Evangelism and Discipleship, a Scriptural Model for Missiology.

First, it is helpful to clarify the term "relational." Hedinger and Wan offer a helpful description:

> Relational in contemporary language translates to "friendly" or "nice." We have in mind the patterns of interaction that exist between people. The relationship we have in mind seeks the best for all involved but are at the same time aware of social expectations. Relationships as we consider it will have friendships, but they might not always be the buddies who enjoy time together. Friendship in the Bible has more to do with faithfulness than emotional satisfaction. Relationship has to do with moving through social networks in a way that respects Biblical expectations in the light of social expectations. It is not just horizontal...God is part of every relationship.[173]

Thus, according to Wan and Hedinger, a disciple is "a person following Jesus (being), being changed (becoming) to be more like Jesus and eager to bring others to Jesus with a kingdom-orientation (belonging)."[174] There is an ongoing relationship between the Triune God and the follower of Christ/disciple (vertical) while simultaneously bringing others to Jesus through a community (horizontal). It just follows that the follower of Christ has an ongoing relationship with the body of Christ (another vertical relationship). "A theology of Gospel transformation begins with transformational change of the individual believer and then extends to his/her network of relationships in multiple contexts of marriage, family, workplace, and community."[175] Relational transformation happens within the context of relationships, primarily with the Triune God extending towards others. Wan itemized his point based on the following Scriptures. Quoting from New American Standard Bible:

a) 2 Cor. 3:18 - But we all, with unveiled faces, looking as in a mirror at the glory of the Lord, are being transformed into the same image from glory to glory, just as from the Lord, the Spirit.

b) 2 Cor. 5:17 - Therefore if anyone is in Christ, this person is a new creation; the old things passed away; behold, new things have come.

c) Acts 3:18 -Therefore repent and return, so that your sins may be wiped away, in order that times of refreshing may come from the presence of the Lord;

d) Gal. 5:22-23 - But the fruit of the Spirit is love, joy, peace, patience, kindness, goodness, faithfulness, gentleness, self-control; against such things there is no law.

---

[173] Enoch Wan and Hedinger, "Transformative Ministry for the Majority Word Context: Applying Relational Approaches" Occasional Bulletin EMS Spring 2018, PDF.

[174] Wan and Hedinger, *Relational Missionary Training*, 13.

[175] Enoch Wan, "Relational Transformational Leadership: An Asian Perspective," "Asian Mission Advance" April 2021, PDF, 1.

e) Phil 1:6 - For I am confident of this very thing, that He who began a good work among you will complete it by the day of Christ Jesus.

Wan and Mikeska define discipleship as "somebody having a personal relationship with Jesus and teaching others to have a passion to live for Christ by loving God and loving others through obediently living out the teachings of the Bible."[176] Figure 9 is the condensed illustration of relational discipleship combining Wan and Mikeska.

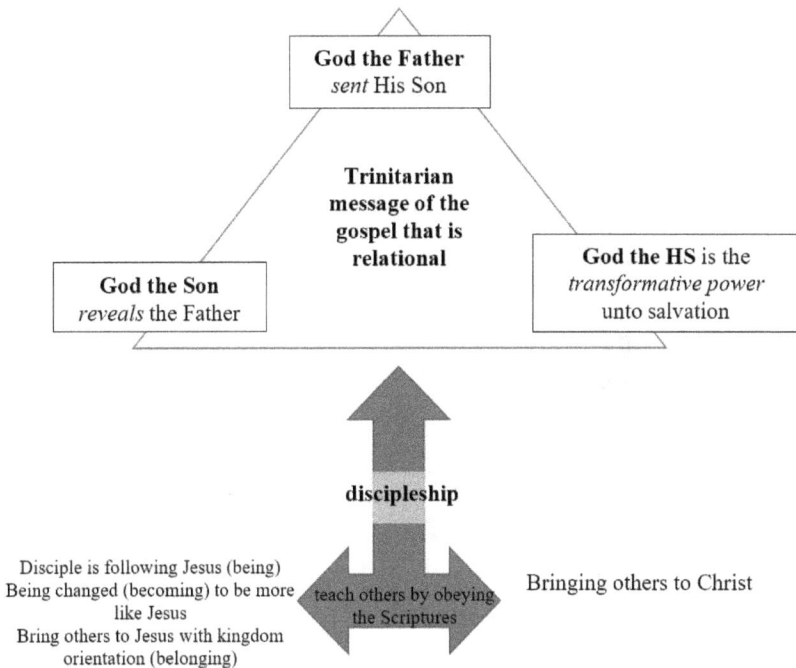

Figure 13 Relational Discipleship by Wan and Mikeska

Steve Murrell, a co-founder of Every Nation Global Family of Churches and author of *WikiChurch,* wrote a section on the book "Discipleship is Relationship." As I note above, he defines discipleship as relationship "first with God (follow), then with nonbelievers (fish), and finally with God's people (fellowship)."[177] He reiterates the importance of authentic relationships. He writes,

We did not begin our discipleship program with a complex system, a list of job descriptions, or an organizational chart, and neither should you. We

---

[176] Wan and Mikeska, *Engaging the Secular World through Life-on-Life Disciple-Making in the British Context*, 1.
[177] Murrell, *WikiChurch,* 69.

began with sincere and authentic relationships. In other words, we actually cared for people. This is how we started, and it continues to be the foundation of all we do.[178]

This account mirrors in practical terms Wan's Relational Realism Paradigm, the vertical relationship with the Father and the horizontal relationship with others not neglecting the community of believers aspect in discipleship. The refrain "Discipleship is relationship" parallels the relational realism paradigm, each relationship equally essential, although primacy with God, and not neglecting one over the other.

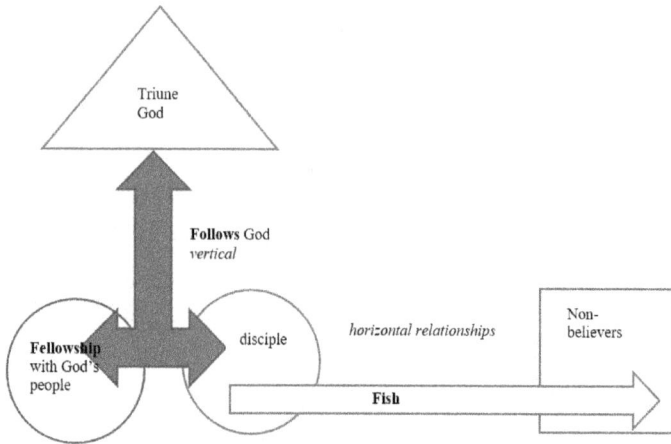

Figure 14 Relational Discipleship by Murrell

This paradigm is Scriptural, as I justified in chapter two, overriding any cultural leanings like the task-based cultures from the global north. I mentioned that engaging cultures from the global north with task-based activities is worth considering for first-generation Filipino missionaries, but it should not end there. Contextualization widely means "identifying the cultural patterns of the receiving people."[179] However, the 21st-century mission is to build bridges of understanding *both* receiving and sending national churches, Wan and Hedinger added. To clarify, "relational emphasis does not eliminate the need for program development... it simply puts the program perspective into its proper relational context."[180] To recall Murrell's statement, "we did not begin with organizational charts...we actually care for people...that is how we started and

---

[178] Murell, *WikiChurch*, 69.

[179] Wan and Hedinger, "Transformationve Ministry for the Majority World Context: Applying Relational Approaches," Occasional Bulletin Spring 2018, PDF, 4.

[180] Wan and Hedinger, "Transformationve Ministry for the Majority World Context," 10.

continues to be the foundation of all we do."[181] Using these three key relationships of discipleship by Murrell, I propose the following diagram to demonstrate another Scriptural basis for relational discipleship.

I quote here John 17 to illustrate Figure 11 (below).

My prayer is not for them alone. I pray also for those who will believe in me through their message, that all of them may be one, Father, just as you are in me and I am in you. May they also be in us so that the world may believe that you have sent me. I have given them the glory that you gave me, that they may be one as we are one— I in them and you in me—so that they may be brought to complete unity. Then the world will know that you sent me and have loved them even as you have loved me.

Father, I want those you have given me to be with me where I am, and to see my glory, the glory you have given me because you loved me before the creation of the world.

Righteous Father, though the world does not know you, I know you, and they know that you have sent me. [26] I have made you known to them, and will continue to make you known in order that the love you have for me may be in them and that I myself may be in them. John 17:20-26, New International Version.

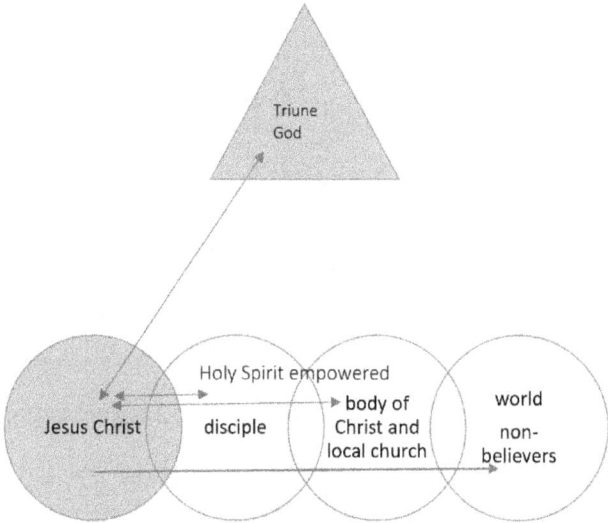

Figure 15 Relational Evangelism and Discipleship

The relational connections from this biblical passage are as follows:

181 Murell, *WikiChurch*, 69.

a) God is relational in being, in this case, persons communicating with one another.
b) God sent His Son Jesus Christ as the economy of salvation, the only way to restore the relationship between man and God.
c) Jesus prayed for his disciples.
d) Jesus also prayed for those who will believe (i.e., future disciples), through their message, to be one with his disciples.
e) Just as the Father and Jesus are one, they (disciples and those who will believe) will be in one.
f) The glory (HS)[182] is with Jesus and with the Father. This same glory will empower them (present and future disciples) to complete unity, just as Jesus and the Father are.

I will now attempt to illuminate the parallelism between the Four E's discipleship principles from Every Nation and the Relational Realism Paradigm.

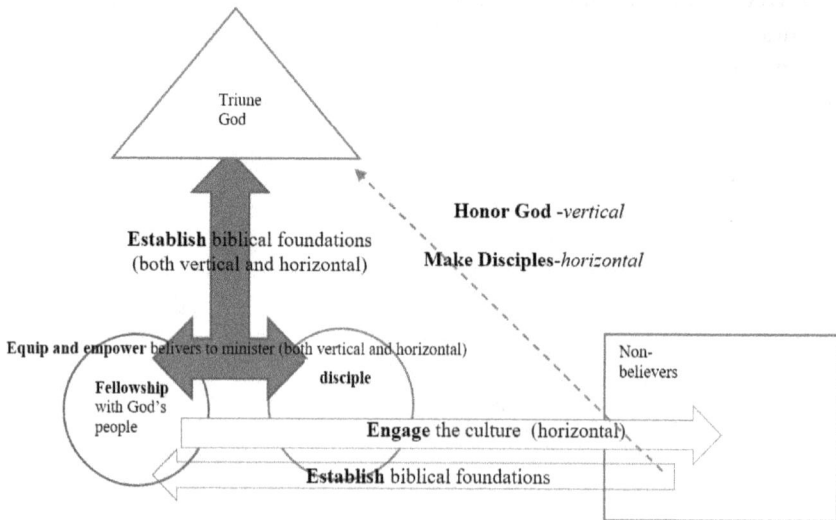

Figure 16 Four E's of Discipleship in Relational Realism Paradigm

The impetus of the organization is to Honor God and Make Disciples. One can immediately recognize the mantra's vertical (Honor God) and horizontal (Make Disciples) elements. Every horizontal engagement should be honorable to God. The connection between the two is inseparable. Likewise, community with other Christians (*koinonia and ecclesia*) is as essential as engaging the culture and vice versa, engaging the culture to bring them into the family of God, hence

---

[182] "The glory Jesus would give to his disciples is similar. It is the glory of oneness with the Father and the Son mediated by the Spirit." Colin G. Kruse, *John: An Introduction and Commentary*, vol. 4, Tyndale New Testament Commentaries (Downers Grove, IL: InterVarsity Press, 2003), 341.

establishing in biblical foundations. The above diagram shows the vertical connection of each of the Four E's, knowing that apart from the vertical relationship with the Triune God, it would be impossible to establish, equip and empower the disciples with the Holy Spirit. According to Murrell, "… all four are essential. If one is removed, the discipleship process breaks down."[183]

In chapter two, Leithart reiterates why our understanding of the Triune God is vital in our understanding of the message of the gospel. It is striking to note how Jesus prayed for unity among the believers and those who will believe through their message; hence, the diagram shows the solemnity and gravity of the Christian community involvement missionally and individually. Since our Triune God is relational, local churches and the Body of Christ unity is as important as "reaching the lost," a common missional term for disciple-making. This unity among the believers is supposed to mirror our relational God. God the Father, God the Son, and God the Holy Spirit are co-partners to redeem the created beings to a relationship with God. When a missionary severs their relational connection from the country they emigrated from or missionary agency, this is an unhealthy and unscriptural mission practice. Just as Jesus did not operate individually but remains connected to the Father and the Spirit, in the same way, mission agencies must continue to nurture and strengthen the existing relationship between the missionary and sending agency (or, if there is an absolute lack of relationship, one must be initiated). There is a certain degree of interdependence healthy for missionaries of all cultures.

In the same way, missionaries need fellow disciples of Christ and the transformative power of the Holy Spirit to mirror this unity that Jesus prayed for in John 17. This level of relationality, Jesus said, is a testimony on its own, a kind of relational evangelism so that the world will know that God loves them. In my opinion, sending missionaries without relational connection to the Body of Christ is putting them in a perilous situation and unhealthy expectations. As a result, we have numerous burnt-out missionary stories, who have neglected their own need for relationships for the sake of the call. They have merely become functionaries for God.

Furthermore, many leadership books apotheosize the "carry the burden" and "leading alone" attitude of normalizing what should not be. Murrell wrote about this highly contagious "Man of God syndrome (MOGS)."[184] He recounts these personality-driven churches with all the contemporary signs of a successful mega-church; edgy interior design in church buildings, beautiful people, stylish super pastors, and the ministry centered around one person. This syndrome may be glamorous or not, but the principle could still be practiced the same way.

Many missionary agencies today carry on the "Great Commission" mindset and highlight its importance as Jesus' last words before his ascension. While that is true, it is imperative not to neglect the three years of modeling *his ways*

---

[183] Murell, *WikiChurch*, 90.
[184] Murrell, *WikiChurch*, 158.

of ministry to his disciples. So, to take the Great Commission out of context is to miss the relational aspect that Jesus modeled for three years before his ascension. In other words, to go and make disciples is to understand life with Jesus. As a result, Wright puts it as "mission proceeds without theological guidance or evaluation."[185] Wan critiques the traditional missiological paradigm that is not only programmatic but deemphasizes the vertical linkage with the Triune God, where "doing" takes dominance over (or even against) "being" and "functionality" trumps "relationality."[186]

As a disciple of Christ, the three key relationships, follow God, fish for men, and fellowship with the local church and Body of Christ, as Murrell stated, happen simultaneously. Additionally, evangelism and discipleship happen simultaneously. Wan's relational realism paradigm of the Great Commission[187] shows continuity rather than a dichotomy.

Table 5 Relational Realism Paradigm and Traditional Missiological Paradigm

A- Relational Realism Paradigm Great Commandment + Great Commission	B- Traditional Missiological Paradigm Great Commission
BEING- vertically God works in us - ⟹	DOING- horizontally God works through us
PERSONHOOD - Christians in Christ ⟹	PERFORMANCE - Christians doing for Christ
MESSENGER - saved/shepherd/sent by Him ⟹	METHOD - making disciples for Him
WITNESSING - by life and living (to serve) ⟹	WINNING - strategizing to win the lost (to save)
VERTICAL - Triune God and His own ⟹	HORIZONTAL - enterprising and managerial
RELATIONAL - vertical + horizontal ⟹	FUNCTIONAL/PROGRAMMATIC - (vertical) horizontal
PROCESS - open ended and unpredictable, ⟹ convergence of tri-systems (i.e.,theo/angelic/human)	PROGRAM - structured plan and procedure

He argues that the traditional missiological paradigms operate separately, emphasizing the output, performance, and winning, section B from the table above. However, Relational Realism Paradigm is not a method. Rather, as Wan and Hedinger remind us,

> It is a reminder that the primary focus for life and ministry has to do with our walk with God and our walk with one another. Technique-focused ministry leads to factory mindset; as if to say, just bring the right raw materials and apply the right methods in the right sequence and you should expect the right outcomes...[188]

This last point is a common 1:1 correlation in evangelism. We know this is not always true for those who have been in the ministry for a long time. Relationalism, Jesus who dwelt among us, is what sustained the great commission.

---

[185] Christopher J.H. Wright, *The Mission of God's People: A Biblical Theology of the Church's Mission (Biblical Theology for Life),* (Grand Rapids,MI: Zondervan, 2010), 19.

[186] Enoch Wan et al., *Diaspora Missions to International Students* (Western Seminary Press, 2019), 11.

[187] Wan et al., *Diaspora Missions to International Students,* 19.

[188] Wan and Hedinger, *Relational Missionary Training,* 216.

John wrote to the church in Ephesus,

These are the words of him who holds the seven stars in his right hand and walks among the seven golden lampstands. [2] I know your deeds, your hard work and your perseverance. I know that you cannot tolerate wicked people, that you have tested those who claim to be apostles but are not, and have found them false. You have persevered and have endured hardships for my name, and have not grown weary. Yet I hold this against you: You have forsaken the love you had at first. Consider how far you have fallen! Repent and do the things you did at first. If you do not repent, I will come to you and remove your lampstand from its place. Revelation 2:1-5 (New International Version).

This text applauds a thriving church in deeds, hard work, and perseverance. They persevered and endured hardships for God and have not grown weary. They have successfully taken the gospel or one could even say "advanced God's kingdom." However, God pointed out this one thing that He holds against the church in Ephesus: "You have forsaken the love you had at first" (Rev. 2:4, New International Version). Leon Morris examines this love:

The condemnation of this church is expressed in one memorable phrase, You have forsaken your first love. It is not clear whether this is love for Christ ('you do not love me now as you did at first'), or for one another ('you have given up loving one another'), or for mankind at large. It may be that a general attitude is meant which included all three ('you do not love as you did at first', Phillips). Forsaken (*aphēkes*) is a strong term; they had completely abandoned their first fine flush of enthusiastic love. They had yielded to the temptation, ever present to Christians, to put all their emphasis on sound teaching. In the process they lost love, without which all else is nothing.[189]

Furthermore, Mikeska argues that,

Modern Christians have a new worldview on Christianity and making disciples. We have created a "build it and they will come" mentality, thinking that if we just build or replant a church, people will come to us. Then we tell our co-workers, neighbors, friends, and family, "If you want to know Jesus, then come to church." When our co-workers, neighbors, friends, and family never come to church, we believe they have rejected Jesus and Christianity, yet the truth is that we have never shared the Gospel with them. We merely told them to come to church.[190]

---

[189] Leon Morris, *Revelation: An Introduction and Commentary*, Vol. 20, Tyndale New Testament Commentaries (Downers Grove, Il: Intervarsity Press, 1987), 65.

[190] Wan and Mikeska, *Engaging the Secular World through Life-on-Life Disciple-Making in the British Context*, 37.

The relational realism paradigm is a timely Christian practice to a world that is relationship deprived. Over the years, churches and missionary agencies have focused on strategic ways to plant churches and make disciples. Due to unmet goals and expectations, one could easily conclude that Christianity is dying. We have attached successful and measurable goals to the status of Christianity when love is the foundation of Christianity. Yet, "*Love* is at the core of Jesus ethic"[191] (emphasis mine). It is rediscovering that we have a relational God who pursued us to restore a relationship with Him. It is what makes Christianity unique from the many religions whose gods are distant and impersonal. "The relational paradigm provides a way to rediscover relationship in Christianity— the essence of Christian faith."[192] For first-generation Filipino missionaries, this value is their contribution to global missions that is Scriptural and reflects an attribute of God.

Relational Mentorship

One of the findings from the participants is the need for mentorship in their new contexts. I now submit my definition of relational mentorship using the relational realism paradigm: Relational mentorship is a transformative and life-giving relationships between mentors and mentees. This relationship is progressive, drawing inspiration from the Triune God's harmonious relationship. Thus, it is able to embrace the challenges presented in an intercultural setting by reflecting God's image in the process.

Here are the underlying assumptions based on the definition:

a) The relational realism paradigm is a conceptual framework for understanding reality based on the interactive connections between personal beings/Beings.[193] The term "relational" in the definition assumes the relational realism paradigm, and the method it suggests is also relational.

b) The Triune God's relationship is harmonious and perfect, while horizontal relationships (relationships between human beings) are progressive. The Triune God's harmonious relationship inspires horizontal relationships between people assuming that mentors have a relationship with God, and that s/he is in a healthy spiritual condition to conduct one-on-one mentorship with a mentee. Because a mentor has a personal relationship with God, s/he understands the concept of *imago Dei*. On the importance of *imago Dei*, see below (chapter seven).

c) Relational mentorship is part of discipleship, fostering healthy relationships within the *koinonia*.

d) A successful relational mentorship is life-giving and transformational for both mentors and mentee.

---

[191] Wan and Mikeska, *Engaging the Secular World through Life-on-Life Disciple-Making in the British Context*, 30.

[192] Wan, *Diaspora Missiology*, 194.

[193] Wan and Hedinger, *Relational Missionary Training*, 14.

e) A mentor understands the need to be interculturally sensitive and competent in relational mentorship. The nature of relationships between human beings is progressive, and God's desire to reconcile involves intercultural settings. I propose a constructive marginality[194] attitude as a way to be a cultural mediator.

In Philippians, Paul addressed our relationships with one another having the same mindset as Christ:

Therefore if you have any encouragement from being united with Christ, if any comfort from his love, if any common sharing in the Spirit, if any tenderness and compassion, then make my joy complete by being like-minded, having the same love, being one in spirit and of one mind. Do nothing out of selfish ambition or vain conceit. Rather, in humility value others above yourselves, not looking to your own interests but each of you to the interests of the others. In your relationships with one another, have the same mindset as Christ Jesus: Who, being in very nature God, did not consider equality with God something to be used to his own advantage; rather, he made himself nothing by taking the very nature of a servant, being made in human likeness. And being found in appearance as a man, he humbled himself by becoming obedient to death— even death on a cross! (Phil. 2:1-8 New International Version).

Scriptural Qualifications for cultural mediators:
a) United in Christ
b) Be like-minded, having the same love, being one in spirit and of one mind
c) Exhibit tenderness and compassion drawn from Christ's love and Spirit
d) Do nothing out of selfish ambition
e) In humility, consider others better than yourselves
f) Not looking at your own interests but the interests of others
g) In your relationships with one another, have the same mindset as Christ

---

[194] "Constructive Marginality can be the most powerful position to exercise intercultural sensitivity", and Cultural Mediator could be accomplished by someone "who could construct each appropriate worldview as needed." See Michael Paige, *Education for the Intercultural Experience*, (Yarmouth, Maine: Intercultural Press, Inc, 1993), 65.

A successful relational mentorship is transformational and life-giving. Relational mentorship maintains a vertical relationship with God and horizontal relationships. I try to summarize this in the diagram below.

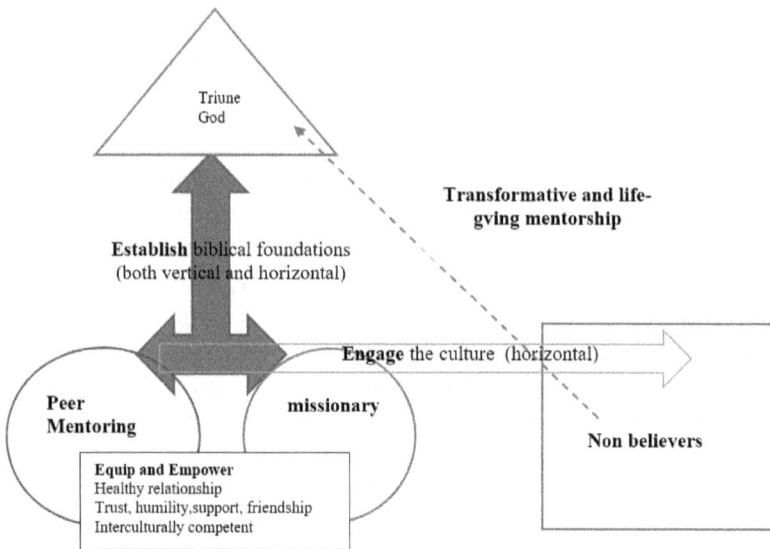

Figure 17 Relational Mentorship

a) Love for others is an outflow manifestation of God's revealed love for His people through Jesus Christ. For relational mentorship to happen successfully, a mentor must have a relationship with God and a healthy state to hold one-on-one relationships with the mentor. This love for others is out of God's love to His people revealed through a relationship with Jesus Christ. As it says in 1 John 4:19, "We love because He first loved us" (New International Version).

b) Love for others means showing no partiality or favoritism. James reminds us of this truth:

> My brothers and sisters, believers in our glorious Lord Jesus Christ, must not show favoritism. Suppose a man comes into your meeting wearing a gold ring and fine clothes, and a poor man in filthy old clothes also comes in. If you show special attention to the man wearing fine clothes and say, "Here's a good seat for you," but say to the poor man, "You stand there" or "Sit on the floor by my feet," have you not discriminated among yourselves and become judges with evil thoughts?" (James 2:1-4, New International Version).

c) In Romans, we are encouraged to show love and kindness on account of the fact that "God's kindness is intended to lead you to repentance" (Romans 2:4b, New International Version).

d) Jesus is the way, the truth, and the life. His way to relational mentorship is life-giving.

> Therefore Jesus said again, "Very truly I tell you, I am the gate for the sheep. All who have come before me are thieves and robbers, but the sheep have not listened to them. I am the gate; whoever enters through me will be saved. They will come in and go out, and find pasture. The thief comes only to steal and kill and destroy; I have come that they may have life, and have it to the full (John 10:7- 10, New International Version).

e) There is a promised encouragement for those who give generously, "A generous person will prosper; whoever refreshes others will be refreshed" (Proverbs 11:25, New International Version).

Summary

The Philippines, as one of the most populated countries in the world, also has a vibrant and growing Christian presence. The nation will soon outgrow the sending of missionaries only within their own region. Through the process scholars call "Reverse Missions," the Philippines will inevitably find themselves commissioning more Filipino missionaries to the global north soon. It is an opportunity involving intercultural challenges. These challenges are solvable through intercultural competency and theological training, most specifically pertaining to the relational realism paradigm as the most compatible missionary framework for missionaries coming from the majority world engaging in diaspora missions.

CHAPTER 4

DIASPORA MISSIONS THROUGH INTERCULTURAL CAMPUS MINISTRY

What made your campus ministry so diverse?

This question speaks volumes to a diverse city such as Seattle, where the city continues to find harmony within tensions brought about by its historical roots and globalization. As mentioned in chapter one, when one of the campus leaders in Seattle visited and observed our campus ministry, two leaders from different campus organizations came with the same question. These organizations have a long-standing record of large group meetings on campus. Their visit to our campus ministry, which is relatively small compared to theirs, led me to believe that perhaps we are doing something right.

When I moved to Seattle from the Philippines to pioneer a campus ministry, I was given the option to start with either international students or locals. Starting with international students would seem a good fit for an international minister like me who recently moved to a new city. It would have been easy to find connection points (living as a foreigner) and potentially minimize barriers in cross-cultural missions. For some reason having an area of focus did not seem to be a priority, or maybe my lack of cross-cultural training pushed me to think, "Well, let us see whom God will bring into our campus ministry." During the first few months of ministry, we had four local students. I met an international student from a local dance studio, and we started spending time together. Bringing her to our small gathering then did not seem to bother her. Learning English was her priority, and the locals seemed very excited to learn from another culture as well. She would come over and bring tasty dishes popular in her country. She started bringing in her classmates, international students from China, South Korea, Taiwan, and Japan. Our international students from different parts of Asia were compelled to speak English rather than their mother tongue. It is advantageous for the group, leaving no one behind in the conversation. As simple as playing board games and sharing meals became our weekly Friday night occasion. Once, we accidentally hosted an International Thanksgiving. Our international students brought dishes to share. We had California maki, Asian noodles, _adobo,_ along with turkey, green beans, and mashed potatoes.

We continue to find our campus ministry becoming a home for both international and local students. For the past eight years of serving as a campus missionary in Seattle, I realized that we were simply faithful to the students God led into our ministry, whether they were locals or international students. I did not create a separate strategy for each one based on their ethnicity. We combined social events, attended one Bible study group using the same story format material, and joined worship gatherings for locals and international students. It was a seamless integration between local and global or international students. So in hindsight, I call it an intercultural campus ministry.

The following section will explain why "intercultural" is an appropriate term for a diverse campus ministry. I will not provide an exhaustive presentation on intercultural and multicultural terminologies but rather expose the tension between the two terms and illuminate why I chose intercultural rather than multicultural as the appropriate term for a truly integrated campus ministry.

A Juxtaposition Between Interculturalism and Multiculturalism

Words such as "multicultural" and "intercultural" are often used interchangeably in dialogues within an organization and institution to reflect equal opportunities in various settings from people of different backgrounds. The terms may appear synonymous, but they have differences in applications and implications. For instance, in research science, education, and policy, "multi-disciplinarity" and "inter-disciplinarity" are used distinctively and differently. "Multi-disciplinarity" study draws on knowledge from different disciplines, but it stays *within their boundaries*. However, "interdisciplinarity" research analyzes, synthesizes, and harmonizes links between disciplines into a coordinated and coherent whole."[195] In politics, The Council of Europe and UNESCO[196] (United Nations Education, Scientific, and Cultural Organization), at the end of the twentieth century, shifted multiculturalism to interculturalism as their official policy and discourse reflecting their international directions and guidelines on educational policies.[197] Halse and Gube, who wrote the article on "The Multiculturalism vs. Interculturalism," quote Sarmento that the move to interculturalism grew out of the tension between the swelling movement of migrants and refugees in Europe and the growing influence of ethnic purity who opposed ethnic diversity. He proposed that multiculturalism encourages ethnic enclaves and strictly culturalized minorities, fostering a threat to national cohesion:

The overriding concern of multiculturalism is how to address these challenges while preserving the distinctive identities of minority groups (Taylor, 2015)... Interculturalism's overarching concern is to address

---

[195] Bernard C. K. Choi and Anita W. P. Pak, "Multidisciplinarity, Interdisciplinarity and Transdisciplinarity in Health Research, Services, Education and Policy: 1. Definitions, Objectives, and Evidence of Effectiveness," *Clinical and Investigative Medicine. Medecine Clinique Et Experimentale* 29, no. 6 (December 2006): 351–364.

[196] Unesco is an international organization that seeks to build peace through international relations in science, education, and culture.

[197] Halse, Christine & Gube, Jan. (2018). The 2018 Kame International Conference "The Multiculturalism Vs Interculturalism: Implications For Asia." Kame is an abbreviation for Korean Association for Multicultural Education.

equities by improving mutual understanding and relations between cultural groups, for example through mutual dialogue, exchange, and policies that recognise diversity but also build social unity and cohesion.[198]

In response to Europe's increasing cultural diversity, rooted in history and globalization, "White Paper on Intercultural Dialogue" was launched to safeguard the future of the society from segregation, the coexistence of majority and minorities, bound together by ignorance and stereotypes. "White Paper on Intercultural Dialogue" argues that "our common future depends on our ability to safeguard and develop human rights, as enshrined in the European Convention on Human Rights, democracy and the rule of law and to promote mutual understanding. It reasons that the intercultural approach offers a forward-looking model for managing cultural diversity."[199]

Furthermore, the prefix "multi" means more than one or many different kinds, and the prefix "inter" means among. Interculturality fosters mutuality, reciprocity, and interaction instead of mere acknowledgment or accommodation of many different kinds of cultures. In the last quarter of the twentieth century, "multicultural" became the official term for political accommodation of minorities[200] but not necessarily equity in rights and privileges. This accommodation of minorities immediately implies that there is a ruling majority.

The term "intercultural" best describes the mutual respect and unity within the diverse campus ministry. The word intercultural fosters integration, interrelation, interconnectedness, interaction, and intermingling of different ethnicities and cultures for social unity and cohesion as opposed to multiculturalism that simply coexists but remains unconnected, unrelated, and unassociated.

What is Intercultural Campus Ministry?

Intercultural campus ministry is an integration of locals and international students into one campus ministry. It has one strategy (prayer and reading of the Scripture), hosts one large gathering, the same Bible study group format, and is church-based. It values both the campus ministry's legacy to reach the next generation and the missional impact of the International Students Ministry. Two scriptural foundations are necessary for ICM, the concept of *imago Dei* (chapter three) and *missio Dei* (appendix 4).

Campus ministries do not only recognize the potential of ministering to college-age students and its impact locally. Alexander Best wrote an article on

---

[198] Halse and Gube. "The Multiculturalism vs Interculturalism," 4

[199] White Paper on Intercultural Dialogue "Living Together As Equals in Dignity" Launched by the Council of Europe Ministers of Foreign Affairs at their 118th Ministerial Session (Strasbourg, May 7, 2008). PDF

[200] *The Blackwell Encyclopedia of Sociology* 2007

its effect globally on the future of missions.[201] Furthermore, International Student Ministries understands its global reach. Most international students who come to faith on our global campuses will return home. Best wrote on Global Campus,

International students belong in and transcend both worlds—at least for a few years. The global campus is world-shaping; it will also be church-shaping, and the diversity of international students can be a chorus, a witness that defies postmodern segregation. It is a diverse harmony that sounds a divine note. We need the global church not just to help us reach the unreached, but to help reach *ours*. Oxford University reports that "student mobility is shifting from a largely unidirectional east-west flow to a multidirectional movement and encompassing non-traditional sending and host countries" International education is becoming polycentric. Global campuses are becoming a worldwide phenomenon.[202]

Intercultural campus ministry is a kind of diaspora missions similar to Wan's characteristics of diaspora for ISM. He pointed out, that "unlike the popular missiology which has a strong distinction between outreach locally (called 'evangelism') and internationally (called 'mission'), in diaspora missiology, there are no territorial distinction; rather integrated 'glocal missions.'"[203]

The glocal mission is a portmanteau of local and global missions happening simultaneously. ISM is a classic example of engaging one's local with a global impact. ISM is practicing glocal missions in terms of reaching the nations represented by international students in the community. They, in turn, go home and impact their nation. While this term was only introduced in the Christian world in the 1990s, the glocal mission has its roots in Acts 1:8, "But you will receive power when the Holy Spirit comes on you; and you will be my witnesses in Jerusalem, and in all Judea and Samaria, and to the ends of the earth."

Roberts commented on the state of the modern church:

We have interpreted it to mean the very opposite of a globally connected world. Our premise has been this: First, we build a strong and big church here. Second, when we're big and strong, we go to our whole country. Third, we go to those near us when we've reached our country — maybe Canada or Mexico. Finally, when we're really strong, we take on the world! Even if it's not explicitly said that way, it is what is practiced. This is not how the church worked in Acts, nor is it the way the world will be transformed for Christ. Acts 1:8 describes glocal in action. This passage was not describing the one-two-three steps but the dimensions in which the church must be working at

---

[201] Alexander Best, "10 Reasons Why the Global Campus Is the Future of Mission," Christianity Today, accessed July 29, 2019, https://www.christianitytoday.com.

[202] Best, "10 Reasons Why the Global Campus Is the Future of Mission."

[203] Wan et al., *Diaspora Missions to International Students*, 30.

all times. It wasn't determining the sequence, but the spheres. This is fascinating because it is exactly what the world has become two thousand years later! The local and the global have come together at many different dimensions.[204]

The concept of glocalization matches the practice of diaspora missions where it is polycentric and multidirectional. Glocalization is a way to understand missions in a globally connected world. The global reach of intercultural campus ministry is the fuel to bring the gospel of Jesus Christ locally and globally simultaneously, where the missionaries and preachers have limitations. It is not anymore the call of an individual, and it has never been. In glocal missions, every believer is a missionary, and that makes ICM, the partnership between the West (local) and the majority world (global), become phenomenal and exponential. Roberts added,

> I've seen the world change from Rome. Mitch Jolly started Three Rivers Community Church three years ago in Rome, Georgia — a fertile field with three community colleges. They now have over 350 in attendance. I recently spoke at a conference for his church. Over 100 college students and people from other churches were present, and it was powerful. These young guys are getting it. Already, they are starting churches. (No one told them they couldn't.)[205]

Consequently, community colleges are the first stop of international students. ICM is glocal. The impact is global, and the engagement is local. As Roberts says, "The story of Acts must remain fresh in our minds. The early church spread as it did because it wasn't an established infrastructure; instead it lay across all the infrastructures of society and infiltrated them with the good news."[206] ICM can potentially impact every fiber of our society (local) and their future society (global, returnees) simultaneously. That is why ICM will thrive in our globally connected world, since universities host every domain of our society.

In conclusion, Roberts quotes Gupta, president of the Hindustan Bible Institute and College in India, on "Global Trends that Influence the Practice of Partnership with Indigenous Mission":

> We still do missions as we did it two hundred and fifty years ago. We want to learn a language; we want to send our missionaries to plant churches; we ignore the presence of an indigenous church movement, the restrictions of nations... The world outside the church is telling us, if we are going to get the bottom line to have its highest return, we must move from the paradigm of independence to interdependence... Missions in the context of globalization must understand that there is greater leverage in building synergy than establishing our banners. It is amazing how secular organizations have

---

204 Roberts Jr., 15.
205 Roberts Jr., 80.
206 Roberts Jr., 83.

understood the concept and developed partnerships that have brought great dividends to their companies... It's time to stop establishing our identity and begin to bring our resources together and work together in the context of interdependence. We must find ways to enter nations from all sides and with every opportunity; we should let the values of the scripture speak through us so that the lost are reached and discipled into the kingdom of God...[207]

The table below is an illustration from Wan's "Missions to the Diaspora" (ISM) as a way to practice "Mission at our Doorstep."[208]

Table 6 Missions to the Diaspora = Mission at our Doorstep

No	Yes
no visa required	yes, door opened
no closed door	yes, people are accessible
no international travel required	yes, missions at our doorstep
no political/legal restrictions	yes ample opportunities
no dichotomized approach	yes, holistic ministries
no sense of self-sufficiency or unhealthy competition	yes, powerful partnership

Like ISM, ICM is not only missions at our doorstep, but missions *help* at our doorstep. ICM sees international students as co-partners in missions and a powerful partnership. It is not only non-territorial because, like ISM they are not reached in isolation but also multidirectional in their participation in missions. It combines the values, plan, strategies, mission, of campus ministry to locals and internationals. One shortcoming of many campus ministries is its partnership with a local church; with International Student Ministries, it is the sustainability of the local chapter when students move to another state or return to their homeland. Intercultural Campus Ministry as a church-based campus ministry strategy could potentially solve both gaps.

Intercultural Campus Ministry Praxis

Intercultural campus ministry values:
    a) Partnership with a local intercultural church.
    b) Student leadership and their involvement in evangelism and peer discipleship.
    c) Daily prayer and reading of the scripture.
    d) Simplicity in Bible study group format so that students of any level can participate.

---

[207] Roberts Jr., 119.
[208] Wan et al., *Diaspora Missions to International Students*, 30–31.

e) Active involvement of the Holy Spirit in welcoming students of all backgrounds reflecting a polycentric and multidirectional approach.

A Diaspora Reflection

In my dissertation, I embarked on this statement: the Philippines' population growth and religious affiliation will put them to become one of the largest Christian communities on the planet by 2050. As "people of faith on the move,"[209] Filipino diasporas will continue to find themselves in unique evangelistic opportunities and challenges. When I moved to Seattle in 2012 to pioneer a campus missionary in the city, I was part of that phenomenon, as were the seven participants for my research, who moved to the different cities in the global north within the last fifteen years. We are part of the Filipino diaspora phenomenon, the first-generation Filipino missionaries who are currently serving in the wealthy cities of the planet. Based on the projections by historians Jenkins and Noll, more missionaries from the majority world will find themselves in this diaspora phenomenon.

Two research agendas served as a starting point to explore the experiences of first-generation Filipino missionaries in the global north. These were to 1) identify the restraining forces/challenges in their local contexts and 2) engage Filipino missionaries in diaspora missions through an intercultural campus ministry.

After synthesizing and reflecting on the answers from the participants, I realized that the restraining forces could be clustered into one major component, the lack of intercultural competency training before the move, something I had also experienced. Restraining forces are solvable gaps with proper intercultural competency training. Chapter three itemized these intercultural gaps, namely: contexts (high and low contexts), trust formation, time orientation and degree of interdependence (individualism and collectivism cultures).

I propose an intervention (see Appendix 5) to engage the participants in intercultural campus ministry. Within this chapter, I argued why I purposely prefer *intercultural* engagement on campus as opposed to the more common term, multicultural. The intervention proposed a specific format for introducing the intervention to first-generation Filipino missionaries in a relational way.

My experience as a campus missionary to the global north established trust and empathy for the participants. They trusted me with their answers that they oftentimes quote "to be honest…" They felt seen and heard.

At the first Peer Mentoring meeting, I shared the themes from their challenges as missionaries. Their faces immediately brightened when they found out that they shared a common struggle. They were excited about collaborating with others, as one commented, "It's like the old times!" and "It is nice to know we are not alone in our situation." I gave them the first twenty

---

[209] Adogame, et al, 2.

minutes just to catch up and connect with each other. They were so eager to learn about the shared context. I saw some of them taking notes during the presentation. Towards the end, they asked for part two, even though my intention was just to have one session. Accommodating this request would provide a platform for connection, competency, and encouragement. The subsequent sessions were agreed to be informal peer mentoring sessions which allowed me to provide a format that hopes to decrease the restraining forces/challenges and increase their driving forces for missions, a process that will continue even after my research. The name "peer mentoring" was suggested to imply equal opportunities and reciprocity within the group.

As the peer mentoring group continued on the intervention, I realized it would take several steps from point A (identify challenges) to point B (engage in diaspora missions). It is crucial to pay attention to these intermediate steps necessary before moving forward. This factor and the Covid pandemic affected my timeline in documenting the results. However, intercultural campus ministry is not lacking potential. One participant recalls that one time they hosted an international student dinner last October 2019, pre-Covid lockdown. She said a student from Zambia came to their church after attending an all-African international students church gathering in Ukraine for quite some time. Maphale, the students' name, said, attending an all-African church is like "patting each other's shoulders," like a monocultural bubble detached from reality, and it is not sustainable. As a result, he became the first African student who crossed cultural boundaries to attend a church that mostly consisted of local Ukrainians. Today, he plays in the worship team and is even married to a Ukrainian.

What is Helpful for Future First-Generation Filipino Missionaries who will Engage in Diaspora Missions in the Global North?

Our theological assumptions determine our approach to missions. My move to the United States as a diaspora phenomenon expanded my understanding of missions. A more traditional understanding of missions as "going" or "sent out" or need-based response determines how one participates in missions. A Filipino coming to the global north as a missionary could spark malicious intentions within the Filipino missionary community and its host city. Immigrants move to wealthy nations primarily to seek job opportunities and support their families back home. The idea of diaspora missionaries to wealthy nations is foreign to both the host city and country of origin. Hence, it is crucial to understand diaspora missions as a divine direction from the Lord. It is Scriptural in its foundation, as exemplified in the gospels. There is a paradigm shift from a monocultural background to an intercultural mission engagement. This shift will lead to intercultural conflicts that are decipherable through a series of intercultural competency training. The best way to navigate intervention is to emphasize the commonalities and manage the differences.

CHAPTER 5

MISSIOLOGICAL IMPLICATIONS

Introduction

I had the privilege of having a meal with Miriam Adeney, a well-known missiologist and prolific writer based in Seattle. Her lecture and speaking engagements span to over five continents. When I arrived at her home, she served me a welcome coffee and snacks, then a rice meal for lunch. We moved from her dining area to her backyard with another set of coffee and banana cookies she made. She lived in the Philippines for a season and most of our conversations revolved around her experiences in the Philippines and my experiences in the Pacific Northwest. Adeney authored over 100 articles and books on Global Christianity, World Religion, and Writing Techniques. Her book, *Kingdom Without Borders: The Untold Story of Global Christianity*, especially caught my attention as the heading of the introduction read, "What I learned from Filipinos."[210]

Tears flowed through my eyes as I read page after page. She narrated a story about Cesar, who taught her early that "America is precious, but so are other places. Home can be anywhere in the world."[211] Her friendship with Melba, God's love displayed through their friendship despite the history of "benevolent assimilation."[212] People Power is another meaningful time in our history when Filipinos used prayer vigils against the government's artillery. It caught the world's attention as a "remarkable example of nonviolent political change with strong Christian input. On every bus I rode, I overheard strangers exclaiming to one another about how God had delivered them,"[213] Miriam recalled. She talked about her friendship with Lisa and Melba and other Filipino friends who taught her new dimensions of worship, community, hospitality, generosity, respect, poverty, and justice and how Filipinos, according to Miriam, continue to bless her. Her words reminded me of God's promise to Abraham, "...and all peoples on earth will be blessed through you" (Genesis 12:3b, New International Version). The call of God in Abraham's life to go from his country, a place of loyalty, his people, a place of cultural identity, and his father's household, a

---

[210] Miriam Adeney, *Kingdom Without Borders: The Untold Story of Global Christianity*, (Downers Grove, Ill: IVP Books, 2009), 7.

[211] Adeney, *Kingdom Without Borders*, 8.

[212] Benevolent Assimilation is "America's Acquisition of the Philippines and Filipino's Resistance," By Stuart Miller, *Benevolent Assimilation: The American Conquest Of The Philippines, 1899-1903*, (Yale University Press, 1982), And Brian D'haeseleer and Roger Peace, "The War Of 1898 And The U.S.-Filipino War, 1899-1902," United States Foreign Policy History And Resource Guide Website, 2016, Accessed December 17, 2021, http://peacehistory-usfp.org/1898-1899.

[213] Adeney, *Kingdom Without Borders*, 11.

place of connection and protection, to a place God will lead and show him. As a diaspora, a foreigner and stranger in another land, the promise is to bless all peoples and all nations. This promise was extended to the children of Abraham by faith. As Paul preached: "Scripture foresaw that God would justify the Gentiles by faith and announced the gospel in advance to Abraham: 'All nations will be blessed through you.' So those who rely on faith are blessed along with Abraham, the man of faith (Gal. 3:7-9, New International Version).

As Filipino diasporas, we emulate Abraham's humility and obedience to God's call by becoming a blessing to all nations in a foreign land. In the following section, I will demonstrate the missiological implications in campus ministry, world missions, and church planting when Filipino diasporas walk away from engaging in diaspora by and beyond practice.

Campus Ministry

My prayer is not for them alone. I pray also for those who will believe in me through their message, that all of them may be one, Father, just as you are in me and I am in you. May they also be in us so that the world may believe that you have sent me. I have given them the glory that you gave me, that they may be one as we are one, I in them and you in me—so that they may be brought to complete unity. Then the world will know that you sent me and have loved them even as you have loved me. (John 17: 20-23, New International Version)

As a campus missionary in Seattle for eight years, the University of Washington became a second home. The university hosts an annual Freshmen Week, where all Registered Student Organizations (RSOs) are entitled to showcase their club and recruit student members. During these times, I noticed a significant number of RSOs that are ethnicity-based. Examples of these are Filipino American Student Association FASA, Chinese Student Associations, Taiwanese Student Association, Association of Black Business Students, and Hispanic Student Dental Association, to name a few (of *many*). While it is beneficial for ethnic groups to preserve, promote, and cultivate their culture in a diverse environment, a study by Mermet Kurtulmus highlights that not all impact from these clubs is positive: "The increasing number of racially/ethnically different students at universities can have negative consequences."[214] The study concluded that diversity climate perception affected the students significantly and negatively. Robust diversity can be a strategic value to an organization, leading to efficiency, collaboration, and problem-solving. However, weak diversity and segregated communities marginalized individuals due to their differences alienating the individual to her/his environment. This alienation hinders undergraduates from belonging to an ethnic group or host city. However, some campus ministries and church

---

[214] Mehmet Kurtulmus, "The Effect of Diversity Climate Perception on Alienation of Students to University," accessed November 5, 2020, https://eric.ed.gov.

planting strategies mirror this type of fragmented ministry through ethnic segregation.

Norton said, "students have been in the frontline of the North America church's missionary outreach, spearheading three eras of missionary advance."[215] Examples of these campus ministries are The Rising Sun and Student Volunteer Movement.

Samuel Mills Jr.(1783-1818) was a first-year student when he founded The Rising Sun in Williams College, Massachusetts. The secret group met twice a week in the afternoon, committed to addressing the throne of grace at sunrise, which later gave birth to Haystack Prayer Meetings. These students were so concerned about world missions that birthed the foundation of the first church-sponsored sending agency in America, the Board of Commissioners for Foreign Missions.[216] Adoniram Judson (1788-1850) was one of the students who emerged from the Haystack Prayer Meeting, and within the next fifteen years, 125 people from Williams College took the gospel to Native Americans.

The growth of the Student Volunteer Movement (SVM) was phenomenal. By 1891 there were 6,200 student volunteers, and 321 had already sailed for missions overseas. SVM was the roaring flame of missionary vision among America's youth with 175,000 students signed the pledge and 21,000 who went overseas."[217] SVM reached its highest point in the 1920 convention when 40,000 students participated in local chapters. However, SVM's steady decline began shortly after, mainly due to theological liberalism and leadership transition. Robert Gallager pointed out that one of SVM's significant contributions was the shift of missionaries sent out from Europe to North America.[218] SVM laid the groundwork for the World Missionary Conference in Edinburgh, Scotland, in 1910, which paved the way for the second half of the century's ecumenical movement.[219] These were students who crossed borders, traveled across oceans, and left what was familiar with the possibility of not seeing their home again. It was part of their legacy. This legacy is slowly fading when we allow fragmented campus ministries in diverse cities. The International Student Ministries saw this opportunity.[220] Why can it not be a unified goal? Fragmented campus ministries like "Asian Christian Fellowship, Black Fellowship, Hispanic Fellowship"[221] retreat to what is familiar and convenient, unintentionally contributing to the marginalization.

---

[215] H. Wilbert Norton Sr., "The Student Foreign Missions Fellowship over Fifty-Five Years," *International Bulletin of Missionary Research* 17, no. 1 (January 1993), 17.

[216] Hunt and Hunt, 34.

[217] Hunt and Hunt, 43.

[218] Robert L. Gallagher, *Encountering the History of Missions* (Grand Rapids, Michigan: Baker Academic, 2017), 270.

[219] Gallager, 270.

[220] Leiton Edward Chinn, "Reflections on Reaching the International Student Diaspora in North America," *Global Missiology English* 4, no. 11 (January 7, 2014), <http://ojs.globalmissiology.org/index.php/english/article/view/1684.> (February 26, 2020).

[221] Pseudonym

To reiterate from a *Christianity Today* article from Alexander Best: "the global campus is world-shaping and church-shaping."[222] The church's challenges on racial unity and reconciliation can be reshaped right on campus, together, not segregated, as we witness the convergence of people from different backgrounds. One participant in this research said, "we need to reach the post-modern students because they will change the narratives of our future."[223] That is true. Like most of the participants, Every Nation Ministries itself embraces the value of reaching this generation. Recent studies are providing us with enough information to receive this mission field as vitally essential.

Furthermore, the campuses in the global north will continue to be the top choice by the internationals for academic pursuits, making its campuses the ideal setting to make the gospel known and change the narratives of our future. It is both a challenge and a potential for any Christian ministry to bring unity through diversity. This challenge is critical in understanding as it holds "the promise of Pentecost, but also the danger of Babel. Only this time, it is several towers, to each its own."[224] I quote Best's concluding statement:

> Christian international students are like the early missionaries to their own countries. They can reach more than just each other; they can reach North American students, who have been immunized from the gospel in their own culture and dialect. In North America, the gospel from the lips of Caucasians is often an offense, and dismissible. But the story told in a foreign accent is a story heard afresh and the diversity of international students, can be a chorus, a witness that defies postmodern segregation. It is a diverse harmony that sounds a divine note. We need the global church not just to help us reach their unreached, but to help reach ours.[225]

Intercultural campus ministry sees each other as co-equals and co-partners in sharing the gospel to others in a polycentric and multi-directional way. It is not linear as a host city to practice hospitality to a foreigner, but a foreigner can be hospitable to its host city and share the gospel to locals and vice versa.

Intercultural campus ministry will also solve the emerging dilemma of second-generation immigrants leaving their ethnic churches. Many ethnic-based churches are putting their hopes on the contribution or influence of second generations to their churches, yet we are faced with the fact that according to Baeq, "...up to 95% of immigrant post-high school churchgoers are projected to leave their churches" shortly after stepping into college.[226] Of course, this is a major dilemma for first-generation ethnic-centered churches

---

[222] Best, "10 Reasons Why the Global Campus Is the Future of Mission."

[223] All interviews are confidential; the names of the interviewees are withheld by mutual agreement." Interviewed by Ria L. Martin. Seattle. March 30, 2021

[224] Best, "10 Reasons Why the Global Campus Is the Future of Mission."

[225] Best, "10 Reasons Why the Global Campus is the Future of Mission."

[226] Daniel Shinjong Baeq, "Mission from Migrant Church to Ethnic Minorities."pdf

and missionaries who put their hope in their second-generation children to bring in the diversity in their congregation.

One participant from my research mentioned the birth of a new local church in a city by a group of new high school graduates who came to know the Lord when they were in high school and moved to a new city for college. There was no church or Christian ministry presence at the university. The most logical thing for them to do at that time is to start one. That is where she came to know Christ. She witnessed it grow to over a thousand students from a small group of thirty students and, over time, reached ten percent of their campus population.[227] This story coincides with the "Holy Club" and other early Christian ministries from the seventeenth century. To keep their devotion to God, they formed an avenue to practice their faith and invite others in the process. It is significant because, in America alone, the least religious generation in America ("Gen Z," as they are called) is also the largest demographic group in the world, comprising thirty-two percent of the global population.[228] This generation has no concept of a world without a smartphone. Gen Z's access to technology is early. A recent study revealed that ninety-five percent of teenagers in America have access to a smartphone.[229] In the past, engagement of the minds was confronted face to face in the cafeteria, university quads, and hallways. Today, this generation is flooded with tons of information and different ideologies on their phones bypassing accountability from their friends, communities, or professors. They can make conclusive statements without rational discourse or verification of facts.

Suppose current campus ministries still think that reaching freshmen students is strategic; they are mistaken. Fifty to seventy percent of young Christians walk away from the church by the time they are in their college years."[230] It was technology that facilitated global evangelization in the past, as stated by IVCF. Technology now facilitates skepticism via mobile devices in the hands of this young generation. This generation is well-informed, well-researched, and can articulate their objections well. Jun Escosar mentioned this same dilemma on relentless campus outreach, particularly a church-based campus ministry in University Belt, Philippines, where many students attend. The fast transition creates a loophole or gap in leadership development and reaching high school seniors became one of their top priorities. It is essential to think through what kind of platforms, including technology, an intercultural campus ministry will undertake, reaching senior high schools and freshmen college students.

---

[227] All interviews are confidential; the names of the interviewees are withheld by mutual agreement." Interviewed by Ria L. Martin. Seattle. March 31, 2021

[228] Sean McDowell, *So the Next Generation Will Know* (Colorado Springs, CO: David C Cook - TBG, 2019).

[229] "Social Media, Social Life Infographic | Common Sense Media," Common Sense, accessed July 26, 2019, https://www.commonsensemedia.org/social-media-social-life-infographic.

[230] J. Warner, "Are Young People Really Leaving Christianity?" Cold Case Christianity, January 12, 2019, accessed July 26, 2019, https://coldcasechristianity.com/.

Engaging high schools should not come as a surprise for us as we have seen many younger participants who walked the streets of America and held up signs "Justice for George Floyd and Breonna Taylor!" Student-led and student-initiated movements are as relevant as today as it was then, and therefore student ministries are equally essential.

Barna's interview with Jonathan Morrow on the challenges of information overload and confusion about truth among Gen Z,[231] he said, "... culture is what people come to see as normal... there are shaping and normalizing forces at work every second of every day in our society, schools, and mobile devices. There is no way for teenagers—or any of us, for that matter—to grow up in a culture and not be shaped."[232]

Furthermore, Ma brought up a concern among new believers on campus that "they did not fit into the new Christian Fellowships that have already existed because they were culturally or socially different."[233] One of the challenges of a fragmented campus ministry is that it is ethnic-based and a dominant culture contributes to the already fragmented ministry. It becomes a never-ending classification and disintegration. In intercultural campus ministry, interculturalism resists the tendency toward any one dominant culture. It is an opportunity to reshape and realign campus ministry to image Christ's church where unity in Christ is the prevailing culture or foundation. Unified in Christ while celebrating diversity. It is finding commonalities among each other as created in the image of God.

Church Planting

For he himself is our peace, who has made the two groups one and has destroyed the barrier, the dividing wall of hostility, by setting aside in his flesh the law with its commands and regulations. His purpose was to create in himself one new humanity out of the two, thus making peace, and in one body to reconcile both of them to God through the cross, by which he put to death their hostility. He came and preached peace to you who were far away and peace to those who were near. For through him we both have access to the Father by one Spirit (Eph. 2:14-18, New International Version).

This text implies that Christ's redemption plan does not end with individual salvation. It only precedes into uniting people groups into one. We have here a

---

[231] Jonathan Morrow is the director of Cultural Engagement in Impact 360, dedicated over fifteen years of his ministry in equipping parents and students on apologetics and biblical faith. He holds a Master of Divinity, Master of Philosophy in Religion and Ethics and a Doctorate in Worldview and Culture from Talbot School of Theology.

[232] Jonathan Morrow, "Building Lasting Faith in Gen Z," Barna Group, last modified July 19, 2018, accessed May 13, 2021, https://www.barna.com/gen-z-qa-with-jonathan-morrow/. "

[233] Ma and Engle, 201.

"portrait of an alienated humanity, then, the portrait of the peace-making Christ and lastly 'the portrait of God's new society.'"[234]

Paul addressed the concept of otherness present among Jews and Gentiles as a distinction and type of division immediately associated as the work of the flesh, instigated by humans, which caused the wall of partition, the dividing wall of hostility between people groups. The gentiles who were once far away, as mentioned in verse thirteen, does not imply far standing from God, but rather in the way that they were "alienated from the citizenship of Israel," outside of a specific people group and "strangers to the covenants of promise," lacking accessibility to God's plan and purposes. Jesus reflected a more polycentric and multidirectional approach in his ministry. By polycentric, it means Jesus is the center that is offered to all peoples of different backgrounds. The outrage from the law experts was mentioned several times in the New Testament when Jesus opened the accessibility to all. Jesus became the fulfillment of the law the Jews could not perfectly fulfill and the known Messiah, unknown to the Gentiles. The two people groups became one in Christ when he abolished the barriers brought about by self-righteousness and condemnation. His love, mercy, and grace meet both. Jesus' plan is to *reconcile both to God*. In the manner of evangelism, our desire to see individual salvation should match our desire to see united people groups reconciled to God.

Furthermore, in church planting, some research indicates that "multiethnic communities that are originally grouped around a common affinity will indeed revert to monoethnic or monolinguistic communities once the ethnic group creates a critical mass. Grant Lovejoy, an International Mission Board orality expert, is similarly finding the same observation among multiethnic churches, which resulted in church splits not based on anger or offense but by language preference."[235] She states that division among cultures is inevitable once one culture becomes dominant. First-generation Filipino missionaries or first-generation immigrants from the majority world might adopt a unilinear approach rather than polycentric if they think reaching Filipinos first will eventually lead other nations. This is not the case, according to Lovejoy. They will often retreat to the familiar, their own culture and language preference. The intention may not be overtly wrong, yet it does contribute to marginalization and pockets of ethnic enclaves adding threat and division within the host city. Likewise, other ethnic-based churches are forced to create their own space if there is no space to be part of the existing churches in their host cities.

---

[234] Francis Foulkes, *Ephesians: An Introduction and Commentary*, Vol. 10, Tyndale New Testament Commentaries (Downers Grove, Il: Intervarsity Press, 1989), 86.

[235] Wan and Casey, *Church Planting among Immigrants in US Urban Centers (Second Edition)*, 84.

Damian Emutche's article, "Church Planting: Past and Present in America,"[236] referred to the book by Albert W. Wardin Jr. - *The Twelve Baptist Tribes in the USA: Historical and Statistical Analysis* as an illustration of the history of division that is not only doctrinal but issues relating to race and class. "Church planters who embrace the homogenous unit principle believe that gathering of people who share an ethnic background, political beliefs, social standing, and so on will be comfortable with one another and therefore, more successful together in forming a new congregation."[237] For instance, The Southern Baptist Convention (SBC), which was primarily a Southern United States white-dominated church, is today, the largest evangelical Christian body in the United States, with members from every ethnic and cultural groups in every region of North America.

SBC also have more missionaries and church planters both in North America and abroad than any other evangelical church. However, *ethnicity is still a crucial factor*. Many of their local churches are still planted along ethnic lines; White, Black, Hispanic, Arab, Asians (Japanese, Koreans, Filipino etc.). The root of this ethnic church planting goes back to early European immigrants who on arrival to the United States, formed ethnic enclaves, and the churches were usually one of the central underpinnings of these new communities.[238]

This early depiction of segregation is a migration pattern, a tradition not necessarily a scriptural orientation that was translated into church planting. As Emutche's main thesis of his article, "Church Planting: Past and Present in America," he said that "... much of the church planting models currently practiced in North America are deeply rooted in the ecclesiological practices of the Euro-American immigrants' traditions rather than a careful biblical reflection on how to reach lost people through church planting." [239] Furthermore, he states that the "the present-day church is too fractured, too theologically and missiologically ill-equipped to reach a diverse society. The church has maintained its homogeneous practices without asking serious questions if it is theologically sound and can be justified in the New Testament."[240]

---

[236] Damian Emutche, "Church Planting: Past and Present in America," published in "Urban Church Planting" of www.GlobalMissiology.org, July, 2012.

[237] Emutche, 9.

[238] Emutche, "Church Planting,"4, quoted from Branson & Martinez, "Churches Culture & Leadership: A Practical Theology of Congregations and Ethnicities," 13. With the recent internal conflicts in the SBC during the past years regarding critical race theory, the consideration of ethnic division and its implications is even more necessary.

[239] Emutche, 2.

[240] Emutche, 11.

Donald McGavran (1897-1990) [241] popularized the homogenous style of church planting, which he practiced in India, where the caste system is highly institutionalized. He emphasized the importance of "becoming a Christian without forcing them to cross-cultural barriers." [242] We still see the effects and live the consequences of that principle to this day. The fallen humanity overlooked our commonality as *imago Dei* and focused its attention on cultural commonality. The goal is finding commonality through diversity, not finding commonality by segregation.

Afe Adogame talked about the "reverse mission," the flow of Christians from the majority world moving to the north, that is irreversible in the future. My only qualm is, will the first-generation immigrant church planters contribute to the already marginalized and fragmented churches in the global north? Or will they reflect the church Jesus describes in Revelation? We are dealing with the aftermath (and in some regions, still in the depths) of "no colored people among white churches." Let us not hope it will shift to "no white people among colored churches." Will we challenge this homogenous unit principle approach that is focused on church growth? Or will we see our understanding and involvement in missions as participation and partnership with God?

Miriam Adeney wrote a section in her article "Colorful Initiatives: North American Diasporas in Mission," responding to the question of how much culture matters. When should culture be a secondary priority? In her response, she narrates an example provided by Frank Epp that took place in the early twentieth century. A German Canadian Mennonite recognized that their church filled up with nominal Christians who prioritized *cultivating their roots* more than their relationship with God. As a result, these Germans decided to send their children to non-denominational schools—consequently, they lost the German language and strong conviction on pacifism, something the group cherished for centuries, but they recovered their zeal and considered "... the trade [to be] worth the cost. These Germans were willing to pay for their ethnicity in order to keep their faith alive into the next generation." [243] I would argue that realigning our cultural identity primarily as *imago Dei* – finding commonalities among diversity will keep our ethnic identity sanctified and take place secondary only to our identity in Christ.

World Missions

He will judge between many peoples and will settle disputes for strong nations far and wide. They will beat their swords into plowshares and their

---

[241] Donald McGavran is a well-known missiologist who popularized Homogenous Unit Principle in church growth as one of his platforms as the Dean of School of World Mission in Fuller Theological Seminary.

[242] Donald A. McGavran, *Understanding Church Growth* (Wm. B. Eerdmans Publishing, 1990), 163.

[243] Miriam Adeney, "Colorful Initiatives: North American Diasporas in Mission," Missiology: An International Review, Vol. XXXIX, no.1 January 2011, PDF. 10

spears into pruning hooks. Nation will not take up sword against nation nor will they train for war anymore. Everyone will sit under their own vine and under their own fig tree, and no one will make them afraid, for the Lord Almighty has spoken. (Micah 4:3-4, New International Version)

This is beautiful utopian imagery, wherein nations will no longer train for war and their artillery is shaped into tools that cultivate rather than destroy. The opposite portrayal of what we often experience in our current reality. In fact, nations rely heavily on their military power to maintain "peace" among nations. The artillery and machinery are indications of a powerful nation seemingly providing harmony. However, that need arises from the fear that someone or others will take over. This is the opposite of what Mic 3:4 says, "everyone will sit under their own vine and under their own fig tree, no one will make them afraid." *This* peace is the kind of peace that Jesus offers. He will arbitrate between many peoples. Jesus, who is for both sides, will make peace between peoples of all backgrounds. Paul's encouragement was to imitate Christ.

Who, being in very nature God, did not consider equality with God something to be used to his own advantage; rather, he made himself nothing by taking the very nature of a servant, being made in human likeness. And being found in appearance as a man, he humbled himself by becoming obedient to death—even death on a cross!

Jesus' gospel of peace brings no threat from others. Christopher Wright expressed in his book *The Mission of God*:

the eschatological vision of redeemed humanity in the new creation points to the same truth. The inhabitants of the new creation are not portrayed as a homogenized mass or as a single global culture. Rather they will display the continuing glorious diversity of the human race through history: people of every tribe and language and people and nation will bring their wealth and their praises into the city of God (Rev 7:9; 21:24-26).[244]

The practice of diaspora missions is a contemporary approach to twenty-first-century missions and a rediscovering of the relationality of our God. Our participation in diaspora missions is not a matter of strategy, but rather a humble realization of our participation in God's mission in any context. It is not a matter of what is convenient or traditional, but receiving the students or people God is leading or bringing into our ministries and our lives. The polycentric or multidirectional nature of Jesus' ministry is his way of bringing the nations to Himself. In that process, he calls for unity as he interceded in John 17, "...that they may be one as we are one—I in them and you in me—so that they may be brought to complete unity. Then the world will know that you sent me and have loved them even as you have loved me" (John 17: 22-23, New

---

[244] Wright, 456–57.

International Version). Jesus prayed for the unity among his disciples as the kind of unity between him and the Father. This unity is a testament to the world of God's love for them. This is an incredible opportunity to participate in the mission of God and intercultural campus ministry is an avenue for that.

Leslie Newbigin awakened the West about the myth of Christendom. The International Missionary Council (IMC) made a resolution for both West and non-West to partner in world evangelization. The West has become equally a mission field as estimated that there would be more missionaries from the majority world than from the West by the end of the twentieth century.[245] We must answer this. Internationals and locals partner together in missions as we embrace this era of globalization.

What about contextualization? One might reason that there exists an increased challenge of contextualizing the gospel to an already diverse community, such as intercultural campus ministry. It is much easier to target a specific people group to contextualize, but an intercultural campus ministry, would be an "endless possibilities of contextualization," as one participant expressed in the interview. Scott Moreau understands the value of contextualization, saying, "without contextualization, people will not connect to Christ in a way that moves their hearts. They will never understand the fullest intent of incarnation."[246] How do you contextualize to diverse cities in this era of globalization? The word contextualization birthed different models and approaches to missions, but it also brought some disagreements and challenges.[247] Moreau quotes David Hesselgrave, who pointed out that the controversy within the term is not yet resolved, "the word has already been defined, redefined, used and abused, amplified and vilified, coronated and crucified."[248]

The dispute in Acts 15 at the Council of Jerusalem did not permit the apostles to settle their dispute through segregation or separate worship gatherings. Instead, they agreed to settle their disputes by living life together. Moreover, after much discussion and debate, Peter brought them back to the fact that God, "who knows the heart, has testified to them by giving them the Holy Spirit just as he did to us, and *he made no distinction between them and us*, cleansing their hearts by faith" (Acts 15:7-9, New English Translation, emphasis mine). Peter reminded them that the God whom they serve made no distinction between them, cleansing them both by faith and the indwelling of the Holy

---

[245] Richard Tiplady, "One World or Many? The Impact of Globalisation on Mission" (Pasadena, CA: William Carey Library) 2003, 258.

[246] A. Scott Moreau, *Contextualization in World Missions: Mapping and Assessing Evangelical Models* (Grand Rapids, MI: Kregel Publications, 2012), 19.

[247] See Enoch Wan's critique to Charles Kraft. He argues with Kraft's *Christianity and Culture* that content is important but not central. Kraft believes that "the process of revelation today is no different that the process of revelation than it was for the biblical authors (2005c, 147)" This orientation is against an important foundation for the evangelical belief that the biblical canon is closed.

[248] Moreau, *Contextualization in World Missions*, 35.

Spirit in them. My proposal for intercultural campus ministry is scriptural in its foundation and approach to missions and focuses on the commonalities of all peoples as *imago Dei*. *Imago Dei* is the pleasantly-placed boundary line, the context God generously created for us. We broke that boundary line when humanity chose to define their own boundaries illustrated in Genesis 3, detailing humanity's rebellion—it led to shame and impaired our relationship with God. God's redemption plan began right after and will fully restore the relationship between God and man one day. Since then, God chose a family, a people group, a nation who will stay faithful to the boundary lines that were set for them, to be a blessing to many nations. Their faithfulness is supposed to be a testament to other nations about God's faithfulness to His people. History proved their attempts were futile and they repeatedly failed, proving that God is the only one who is faithful. When Jesus inaugurated his ministry as the new Adam, he did not choose another people group. Instead, he continued his ministry to the chosen people in Galilee, where nationalities collide, but extended that ministry beyond a singular group. The plan was always for the inclusion of all nations in the international family of God.

Intercultural campus ministry as a diaspora missions' praxis reflects Jesus' ministry in the gospels. It is both centripetal in its theology, everyone as created in the image of God and centrifugal, bringing peace in their participation in mission wherever they are. A scriptural polycentric and multidirectional approach to missions.

David Bosch, in *Transforming Missions*, says,

> I have suggested that Jesus had no intention of founding a new religion. Those who followed him were given no name to distinguish them from other groups, no creed of their own, no rite which revealed their distinctive group character, no geographical center from which they would operate. The twelve were to be the vanguard of all Israel and, beyond Israel, by implication, of the whole ecumene. The community around Jesus was to function as a kind of *pars pro toto*, a community for the sake of all others, a model for others to emulate and be challenged by. Never, however, was this community to sever itself from the others."[249]

Our concern should be the kind of unity Jesus prayed for his disciples and for those who will believe. This unity between people groups will bring the world closer to God—an oft-neglected part of our participation in the *missio Dei*. In conclusion, Bosch reiterated that,

> ... mission is more than just an activity of God but an attribute of God. "It is not the church that has a mission of salvation to fulfill in the world; it is the mission of the Son and the Spirit through the Father that includes the church" (citing Moltmann). Mission is thereby seen as a movement from God to the world; the church is viewed as an instrument for that mission. There

---

[249] Bosch, 43.

is church because there is mission, not vice versa. To participate in mission is to participate in the movement of God's love toward people, since God is a fountain of sending love.[250]

The Bigger Picture

The Philippines will become the fourth largest Christian community on the planet by 2050, Jenkins claimed. Filipino diasporas' massive dispersion began in the 1970s, making them one of the largest groups of immigrants on the globe today. Migration and their Christian affiliation propel them to propagate their faith wherever they go. Despite the marginalization most of them experience in their workplace, as testified by OFWs, their positive traits fuel them to endure, specifically their relationality. Their relationship with God inspires them to persevere, and a healthy relationship with others enables them to thrive in their workplace.

When the first-generation Filipino missionaries moved to the global north, they experienced dissonance in their mission practice: "Why is it not working here?" They considered that maybe relational discipleship only works in the Philippines or other relational cultures. However, this is untrue. The relational realism paradigm is Scriptural. I presented in chapter two that our Triune God is relational and his ways to redeem the world are also relational. God desires relationships with His created beings restored to Him and to one another. To be relational is Scriptural, it transcends all contexts, including the global north. Intercultural competency helps us understand our differences, but relational realism is the *corrective lens* applied to see that the principle encompasses all peoples of all cultures. In other words, the link is the relational realism paradigm.

Chapter four expanded on the potential of intercultural campus ministry as world-changing and church-shaping towards diaspora missions. Consequently, the top international students' countries of origin come from the Majority World, where the largest Christian communities reside and are culturally relational.[251]

---

[250] Bosch, 392.

[251] The top three international students countries of origin are China, India, and South Korea. They all fall into the relationship-based trusting scale from Erin Meyer's culture map tool.

Additionally, Newbigin talked about the partnership between the West and non-West in reaching North America. The West and the Majority world partnership is mirrored through Intercultural Campus Ministry towards diaspora missions to become an intercultural church. The diagram below encapsulates the impact of intercultural campus ministry towards an intercultural church.

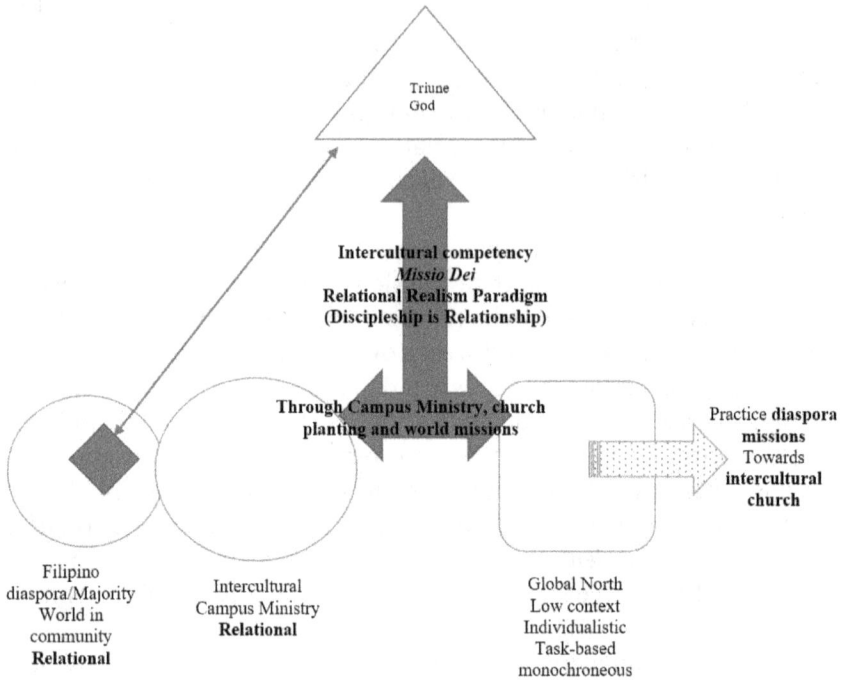

Figure 18 Intercultural Campus Ministry Towards Diaspora Missions

Summary

In this section, I emphasized the missiological implications of my study into three major components: campus ministry, church planting, and world missions.

Campus ministry: I pointed out that the ongoing fragmented campus ministries actually contribute to the marginalization and alienation patterned after university student organizations. This method is contrary to the legacy of past campus ministries who pioneered cross-cultural missions. The global campus is where international and local students converge thus has massive potential for world-shaping and church-shaping. I concluded with the ever-increasing need to reach the next generation, including second-generation immigrants and senior high school using technology as a creative tool in engaging these students.

Church planting: Like campus ministry, most churches in diverse cities face the dilemma of breaking away from a monocultural church. Even though it is beneficial to plant a church with your own kinsmen initially, it will be disadvantageous in the end, not caused by theological disagreements but by the perception of otherness by its host city and language preference. This behavior of gathering one's kinsmen is a migration pattern that is not scriptural when adopted as a church planting strategy. Following Adeney, I considered questions around the importance of cultural identity and its preservation in the church. For missionaries from the majority world who are coming into the global north, we are faced with both opportunities and challenges. Will we become a church that has no whites among the colored?

World missions: This section emphasized the significance of understanding diaspora missions as Christians humble participation in God's redemption plan. His plans go beyond individual salvation but peace among nations to reconcile the world to Himself. He chose the unity between people groups as one of the ways to prove that God loves the world. Newbigin saw the importance of partnership between the West and non-West in world evangelization. Bosch highlights the heart behind missions. It is more than an activity but an attribute of God.

I presented how ICM fits into the crevices and gaps that will serve as a linking platform to practice diaspora missions in all these three components.

CHAPTER 6

CONCLUSION

In the opening chapter of this book, we presented the unique opportunities for first-generation Filipino missionaries on account of the shifts in global Christianity, making the Philippines one of the largest Christian communities on the planet by 2050, according to historians Jenkins and Noll. This global phenomenon positions Filipinos in unique missionary opportunities as well as challenges. As a Filipino diaspora in the United States, I experienced a paradigm shift in understanding and engaging in missions through intercultural campus ministry, which paved the way for my dissertation as explained in the introduction in Chapter 1.

In chapter two, we enumerated studies by several scholars concerning the field of diaspora missiology. This framework is Scriptural and practiced by other ministries, demonstrating that Filipinos have successfully lived and modeled diaspora missions. Diaspora missions are meant to reach other nationalities beyond our kinsmen. Moreover, it is polycentric and multi-directional rather than the more traditional "West to the rest." This missiological paradigm shift enables Filipino and other missionaries from the majority world to participate in missions, including to wealthy nations. This phenomenon is not based on strategy, but on a recognition of and partnership in God's initiative. A reminder for us missionaries, missionary agencies, and churches that missions is first and foremost *missio Dei*—His mission. Therefore, our mission practices must reflect our relational God. Our engagement and Christian practice must be relational, covering three key elements: relationship with God, the community of believers, and the world. Relational realism serves as the corrective lens to engage in evangelism and discipleship. As a result, the practice of relational discipleship is not just for Filipinos nor relational cultures. It is Scriptural and reflects our Triune God.

Many campus ministries today continue the legacy of reaching the next generation. The birth of ISM was an answer to reach the nations that are within the nation's borders. ICM combines these two valuable ministries into one local campus ministry where locals and international students are integrated and interconnected into one local campus ministry. Today, we face yet another opportunity in diaspora missions engagement through intercultural campus ministry—a gateway to becoming an intercultural church that will model Christ's church that is genuinely every tribe, tongue, and language. In the previous chapter, we demonstrated the missiological implications along three points: campus ministry, world missions, and church planting. ICM would solve most of the church planting gaps in North America, continue the legacy of reaching the next generation while seeing the next generation from the majority world as partners and co-laborers, and church planting beyond winning souls proceeding to reconcile nations. This approach displays God's love to the world through the unity of Gpd's people.

Seven first-generation Filipino missionaries participated in the research inquiry. The participants are all first-generation Filipino missionaries from the Philippines who served in their home country for at least ten years before moving to the global north. They are currently serving in Ukraine, Germany, Belgium, Canada, London, and Australia. Even though they were seasoned missionaries in the Philippines, findings after the interview showed that most of the restraining forces or challenges experienced in their contexts are due to a lack of intercultural competency training. Most of these challenges revolve around engaging the community and working with a diverse leadership team. In engaging a community, culture is *always* at play, whether the missionary is aware of this fact or not. Each culture, whether individualistic or collectivist, understands and values time, relationship, and trust differently. Consequently, cultures in the global north operate differently from Philippine culture. Their frustration expressed in "Why is it not working here" is not necessarily that the principle of discipleship is wrong (i.e., engage the community), but that when engaging the community in their context, it requires understanding the culture they are in and is solvable through intercultural competency training. Awareness of cultural differences is not enough, however. Otherwise, difference-based missionary training models, like those we considered above, would be much more effective.

Peer mentoring was established immediately after the interview to serve as a platform for competency (intercultural and theological), connection, and encouragement. As a reflective action researcher, we decided to delay the intervention until after several peer mentoring sessions. An intervention related to intercultural campus ministry is not hard to propose to the participants since they already possess the value to reach the next generation and the desire to reach the nations represented in their city. In fact, it showed in the interview how some of them practice this by hosting parties and hanging out with international students. One key factor of the intervention is to ensure that the local students are involved and interconnected with the international students.

Marginalization is a reality that first-generation Filipino missionaries experience in the global north. Western cultures often see others initially as a threat, a vantage point from host cities present in the global north. Our presence in the new city as first-generation Filipino immigrants is first perceived initially as a threat. Consequently, the more we gather with our kinsmen, the more it breeds threat, an essential element in missional encounters emphasized by Woods.[252] It creates a destructive cycle of marginalization contributed by both the immigrants and the host city. We re-introduced the redemptive analogy of _kapwa,_ the Tagalog word for others and how it is Scripturally aligned. The presence of marginalization should not be a factor in whether we are to send missionaries to a specific country or not. The healing of nations happens when nations interact interculturally, not separately.

Closing the Loop on Ria's Story

"Kay" entered the story in chapter two as the student I met in a dance studio and the first international student who invited herself to my daily activities without any reservations. She came to know Christ through our intercultural campus ministry and invited many of her friends from school to our gatherings. Meeting someone from China as one of the first significant interactions I had as a Filipino campus missionary in Seattle was a surprise. Even though I prayed that God would bring in students, Kay was someone I did not anticipate. Nor was I most excited about her. Engaging with Chinese students is something I thought I would struggle with the most. Growing up in the Philippines, I have always been aware of the political tension between the Philippines and China. I have heard of stories of maltreatment the Filipinos experience working for Chinese employers, and through the years, I had unknowingly and unintentionally developed a prejudice against them.

God exposed that when He brought this student into my life. Kay, who now introduces me as "my mom in Seattle," who invited me to come to her graduation to represent her family who could not get a visa from China, who still calls me whenever she is troubled, and sent me a box of Asian snacks she ordered from China during the pandemic. She brought so much healing into my heart as she embraced me into her life. Oftentimes, we associate mission to mostly reaching the lost souls, but God is concerned with the lost souls as much as his already redeemed people. The mission is not just an activity Christians do _for_ God but also an interaction between God, the missionary, and the people (of any background) whom He chooses to bring into the picture. Like Melba to Miriam and all the other diaspora stories, God's love overflows through people groups despite the growing hate and prejudice surrounding us. Could it be that this has been God's plan all along? Jesus prayed for the unity between the disciples and those who will believe in the future, the same unity that the Father and Son have so that the world will know the Father loves them. The kind of unity impossible to attain by human effort and possible only with the Holy Spirit. More than ever, we need to be a generation that seeks the power of

---

[252] Paul Woods in "God, Israel, The Church and the Other: Otherness, as a Theological Motif in Diaspora Mission" in _Scattered and Gathered: A Global Compendium of Diaspora Missiology_ (Oxford, England: Regnum Books International, 2016)..

the Holy Spirit in our lives in bringing peace and healing in this world and His involvement in our own healing and participation in missions as well.

For Filipinos scattered across the globe, Jollibee is a home away from home. Jollibee is the number one fast-food chain in the Philippines, and it is known for its famous Chicken Joy (fried chicken) topped with gravy, sweet spaghetti, traditional *palabok* (noodle dish), and its famous *halo-halo* dessert. Jollibee embodies Filipino cultural values. It is a venue of choice for various celebrations such as baptisms, birthdays, and weddings that bring out the Filipino values of family, togetherness, and care. Jollibee is well visited internationally by Filipinos who now work or live abroad. They travel from miles away and wait in line for hours for a taste of home—truly a nostalgic experience. It has become a place of safety, familiarity, connection to kinsmen, and refuge for Filipinos living as foreigners. As much as I love Jollibee and bring my friends to it, unless they are Filipino, the nostalgic experience is just one way—it only caters to me. My non-Filipino friends might never visit it independently, no matter how much they like the food, because it is a cultural experience. When Christians prioritize cultural experience in mission, church planting, or campus ministry, it becomes exclusive. This is not a call to abandon culture. It has its place in our homes, language, practices, traditions, and clothing. However, we must be careful in using the church to preserve or prioritize a single cultural identity rather than create a place for all cultures to worship God. It is misplaced cultural loyalty. On wrestling with the issue of salvation versus what were mere cultural practices in Acts 15, Allen Yeh concluded that "culture trumps peripheral theology, but core beliefs trump cultural practices."[253] Yeh quotes Duane Elmer, who says,

> The missionaries who went out after World War II were committed to bringing the gospel of Jesus Christ to every tribe, tongue, and people. Mission was defined in terms of tasks to be accomplished: language study, translation, evangelism, church planting, discipleship, medical work, education, and other ministries. While most of these require some relationship with people, the emphasis was on getting the job done.[254]

I can find many ways to critique their efforts on being task-oriented. However, the level of commitment to bring the gospel of Jesus Christ to every tribe, language, and people through language learning, medical work, education, and non-profit organizations birthed creative access to tough nations, thereby reaching the unreachable people groups is an admirable sign of devotion. Their vision emanates from what John foresaw in Revelation, "After this I looked, and there before me was a great multitude that no one could count, from every nation, tribe, people and language, standing before the throne and before the Lamb. They were wearing white robes and were holding palm branches in their

---

[253] Allen Yeh, *Polycentric Missiology: 21st-Century Mission from Everyone to Everywhere* (Downers Grove: IVP Academic, 2016), 3.

[254] Yeh, 13.

hands" (Rev. 7:9, New International Version). A church of Christ too numerous to count from all walks of life. Today, we have this opportune time when nations are brought together on campus and in our neighborhoods. First-generation Filipino missionaries or missionaries from the majority world who will find themselves in this unique opportunity among other nations in the global north can emulate this same dedication. We can join the call of Abraham to leave our source of connections, cultural identity, temporary refuge, and place of loyalty to God's call to a larger family, where kinship is extended as far as His forgiveness, mercy, and love abound through the blood of Christ.

Adeney quotes Justo González, a celebrated Cuban theologian,

> Our music and our worship must be multicultural, not simply because our society is multicultural, but because the future of God is calling us is multicultural—not just so that those from other cultures may feel at home among us but also so that we may feel at home in God's future.[255]

To rephrase this quote: our music and worship, and I say, we ourselves, must be intercultural, for the future God into which God is inviting us is itself intercultural.

"You are worthy to take the scroll
and to open its seals,
because you were slain,
and with your blood you purchased for God
persons from every tribe and language and people and nation.
You have made them to be a kingdom and priests to serve our God,
and they will reign on the earth."

Then I looked and heard the voice of many angels, numbering thousands upon thousands, and ten thousand times ten thousand. They encircled the throne and the living creatures and the elders. In a loud voice they were saying:

"Worthy is the Lamb, who was slain,
to receive power and wealth and wisdom and strength
and honor and glory and praise!"

Then I heard every creature in heaven and on earth and under the earth and on the sea,
and all that is in them, saying:

"To him who sits on the throne and to the Lamb
be praise and honor and glory and power,
for ever and ever!"

Rev 5:9-13

---

[255] Adeney, "Colorful Initiatives." PDF, 20.

APPENDIX 1

RESEARCH DESIGN AND PROCESS

Introduction

Given the background of this study and the researcher, participatory action research provides access to the inquiry, empathy to the purpose, and appropriate interpretation/analyses of data. The author also is a reflective researcher. She assisted and facilitated the intervention within the setting for improvements in a dialogical manner.

Action research (AR) is a research methodology widely used by practitioners who are seeking solutions to improve or affect change in their current setting. The context is the space providing the researcher to conduct the intervention. Many researchers find AR helpful "because it integrates theories and research into practice."[256] Action research, in a nutshell, is research with action, focusing on its local problems. It begins by trying new strategies and determines the consequences.

Kurt Lewin (1890-1947), one of the founders of AR, wanted to connect national problems with local problems, like racism and poverty. He believes that research and theory should lead to action, specifically social improvements.[257] AR serves various purposes, from as simple as improving a student-teacher relationship in a classroom to complex issues as revising laws.[258]

When considering a change in a setting, Lewin's Force Field Theory is practical. The status quo is called quasi-stationary equilibrium, where the driving force (forces for a change) and the restraining force (forces against change) are roughly equal that keeps the status in an equilibrium state. Both these forces are either motivated, influenced, or guided by these factors:

   a) Physical forces (physical abilities like a location of the building, technology)
   b) Psychological forces (attitudes, motivation for change, habit, personal or religious beliefs)
   c) Group forces (school culture, social attitudes such as stereotypes of groups of people)
   d) Others

---

[256] johnson And Christensen, *Educational Research*, 11.

[257] Johnson and Christensen, 59.

[258] Brian Stevenson is Harvard Law graduate and founder of Equal Justice Initiative. His non-profit law office represents marginalized and poor victims of injustices. He uncovers unjust and inhumane practices inside prison cells experienced by incarcerated youth due to misapplied laws. He had successfully challenged some of these existing laws and narrated in his recently published book *Just Mercy*.

By conducting a Force Field Analysis, the researcher will be able to re-ignite the forces pushing for change and identify resisting forces.

John Dewey is another major influence in action research. As an educator, philosopher, and psychologist, Dewey "has great faith in the power of education to improve society."[259] He thinks that people are problem solvers. Doubt is the key to start thinking and planning ways to make improvements. For Dewey, a scientific method is just another name for inquiry, and daily inquiry happens in our lives centered around values. He often refers to himself as an "instrumentalist," meaning that each one should try new approaches to problematic situations to determine what works better. Dewey is a value-based pragmatist.

Beth Grant defined AR akin to Lewin's description. She emphasized that "More proponents of AR challenge the traditional social science claim of neutrality and objectivity, proposing a 'collaborative inquiry' by all participants instead, often to engage in a sustained change in organizations, communities, or institutions)."[260] In this process, the research and the participants are *co-inquirers* in the solution-focused investigative process.

Even though proponent Ernest Stinger argues that "AR may not meet the stringent criteria and rigor for scholarly scientific research,"[261] Dewey believes otherwise, stating that a scientific method is simply another term for inquiry. As an action researcher, this process has allowed me to be a reflective researcher, active listener, and empathic observer. In sum, as Gilbert states: " AR is more democratic, empowering, and humanizing than traditional scientific research."[262]

Methodological Design

This qualitative study will adopt Dewey's Single Loop Dynamic Cycle (see figure below), incorporating Lewin's Force Field Analysis Theory.[263]

[259] R. Burke Johnson and Larry Christensen, Educational Research: Quantitative, Qualitative, and Mixed Approaches (Thousand Oaks, California: SAGE, 2017), 61.

[260] Gilbert, *Missiological Research: Interdisciplinary Foundations, Methods, and Integration*, ed. Marvin Gilbert, Alan R. Johnson, and Paul W. Lewis (William Carey Library Publishing, 2018), 239, citing Marshall and Rossman 2006, 6-7.

[261] Gilbert, 240.

[262] Gilbert, 240.

[263] Johnson and Christensen, *Educational Research*, 59 and 69.

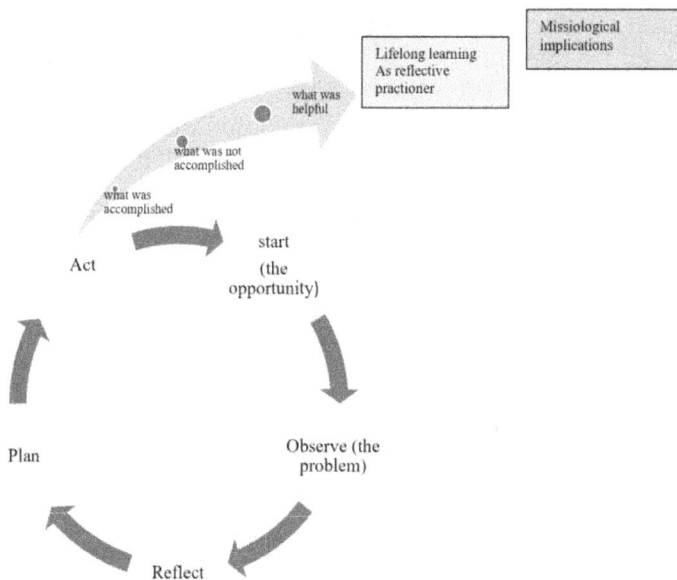

Figure 19 Single Loop Dynamic Cycle

Research Process and Procedures

The research processes and procedures based on Dewey's Single Loop Dynamic Cycle followed the following steps:

Start

In this phase, the researcher verified an initial list of first-generation Filipino missionaries (pastors and campus missionaries) currently serving in the global north overseen by Victory Philippines missions director.

The opportunity: I informed all willing participants that this research would benefit first-generation Filipino missionaries currently serving in the global north and future first-generation Filipino missionaries who want to engage in diaspora missions. All participants will remain anonymous throughout this dissertation.

The initial list of participants and their following contexts are the United States: (2 couples), Australia (1 couple), Spain (1), Canada (1), London (2), Germany (1), Belgium (1), and Ukraine (1). Out of ten potential participants, seven took place in the study.

Upon approval from the Institutional Review Board (IRB), the researcher contacted each potential participant for this research. The conversation began with casual introductions, followed by background information about her ministry in the United States and the dissertation proposal.

After signifying their interest in the project, the researcher sent the consent form and a brief overview of diaspora missions. In the email, participants were informed to confirm their interest by signing the consent form and providing a schedule for the interview. Once the researcher received a favorable reply, she scheduled the individual interviews. I sent the interview guide questions before the scheduled interview. Each interview (in a video call format) lasted ninety minutes. During the interview, I reviewed the consent form and emphasized their right to withdraw from the study at any time.

Observe

This process is between the researcher and the Filipino missionaries.

a) The researcher designed an interview guide that will forecast data needed to answer research questions from chapter one. Each participant received a copy before the scheduled interview. A copy of the interview guide may be found in Appendix 1.

b) Patton's classification of interviews[264] is both conversational and situational. This interview guide approach allows me to discuss specific topics and have room to explore other potential themes.

c) The interview commenced one week after the approval of this dissertation proposal by IRB.

d) Transcriptions of all interviews were made possible by a paid software called rev.ai. The researcher listened to the audio recording while reviewing the transcription. A copy of the transcription was sent to the participants to validate the accuracy of the transcription and inform of any corrections they may have.

e) A short debriefing took place right after the ninety-minute interview reassuring the participants of their anonymity, appreciating their time for the research and group intervention as the second interview.

Reflect

This process provided space for the researcher to reflect and interpret the data collected after the interview.

The researcher reviewed the transcriptions at least three times and looked for emerging themes identifying the restraining forces in their contexts.

---

[264] Johnson and Christensen, 236.

Plan

Based on the transcription, the researcher identified the following, using Lewin's Force Field Analysis:
   a) What are the restraining forces or forces supporting the status quo based on these three classifications?
      a.   Physical forces
      b.   Group forces
      c.   Psychological forces
   b) What are the driving forces that call for change?

Act

The intervention.
   a.) Present some of the restraining forces from the findings and collaborate for solutions.
   b.) Introduce Intercultural Campus Ministry to the participants.
   c.) As co-inquirers, discuss the intervention.
   d.) Address the consequences of the intervention.

Action Research Journal

This research process ends with documenting the following elements as a Reflective Practitioner and Lifelong learner by Schön.[265] After the intervention, the researcher reflected on questions such as:
   a.) What was accomplished?
   b.) What was not accomplished?
   c.) What is helpful for future first-generation Filipino missionaries who will engage in diaspora missions in the global north?
   d.) What are the missiological implications?

Technique

Beth Grant discussed the weaknesses of AR in chapter forty-three of *Missiological Research*.[266] I will itemize each weakness and address these weaknesses to maintain the validity and reliability of this research.

Lacks Academic Research Rigor

In qualitative studies, the researcher is the sole instrument of the study and the primary mode of data collection[267] while maintaining rigor in the process.

---

[265] Johnson and Christensen, 69.
[266] Gilbert, *Missiological Research*, 240.
[267] Brigitte S. Cypress, "Rigor or Reliability and Validity in Qualitative Research: Perspectives, Strategies, Reconceptualization, and Recommendations," Dimensions of Critical Care Nursing 36, no. 4 (August 2017): 253–263, accessed January 18, 2021

Brigitte Cypress[268] began her article by identifying rigor versus trustworthiness, both important for qualitative research. For Cypress,

> Rigor is simply defined as the quality or state of being very exact, careful, or with strict precision or the quality of being thorough and accurate. The term qualitative rigor itself is an oxymoron, considering that qualitative research is a journey of explanation and discovery that does not lend to stiff boundaries.[269]

Academic rigor is expected in qualitative research to combat subjectivity and ensure the reliability and validity of the research. To reiterate Cypress's remarks, rigor in qualitative studies is oxymoronic. Lincoln and Cuba,[270] proponents of the Naturalistic method of scientific research, use a more appropriate term, "trustworthiness." Trustworthiness for the authors simply asks, "How can an inquirer persuade his or her audiences (including self) that the findings of an inquiry are worth paying attention to, worth taking account of?"[271] The goal of the study is trustworthiness and something to be judged during and after conducting the research. The four traditional criteria are truth value, applicability, consistency, and neutrality. They use analogous terms within the naturalistic paradigm, credibility, transferability, dependability, and confirmability.[272] Standards and checklists created a long list of techniques established by qualitative researchers, and for this research, I used peer-debriefing (reviewer's lens), members checking (participant's lens), and reflexivity (researcher's lens). Peer debriefings were participated by three staff from Victory's missions department. Findings from the research were presented to them. Reflexivity, through action research journaling, answered questions on what was accomplished, what was not accomplished, and how the research was helpful for future first-generation Filipino missionaries in the global north. Member checking asked the participants to validate and review the transcribed interview for accuracy, not on interpretation nor analysis of data to avoid manipulation.

Lacks Clearly Defined Recognized Methodologizing (Processes)

Given the nature of how AR was founded, the seeming lack of an exact methodological process is the space that allows the researcher and participants

---

https://journals.lww.com/dccnjournal/Fulltext/2017/07000/Rigor_or_Reliability_and_Validity_in_Qualitative.6.aspx.

[268] Brigitte Cypress Edd, Rn, Ccrn, is an Assistant Professor Of Nursing, Lehman College and The Graduate Center, City University Of New York.

[269] Cypress, "Rigor or Reliability and Validity in Qualitative Research."

[270] Yvonna Lincoln and Egon Guba (1924-2008) are co-authors of *Naturalistic Inquiry*, proponents of Naturalistic mode of inquiry, an alternative scientific method of research than the more popular "rationalistic," a paradigm shift in scientific research.

[271] Yvonna S. Lincoln and Egon G. Guba, *Naturalistic Inquiry* (Newbury Park, CA: Sage publications, 1985), 290.

[272] Lincoln and Guba, 290–331.

to engage in social issues. Social issues are group behaviors and norms that are complex and dynamic. Dewey argues that "AR is more democratic, empowering, and humanizing than the traditional scientific method."[273] Finding a simple solution to a simple problem is in itself an inquiry. Dewey refers to an inquiry as a scientific observation. Just because the process is simple, it does not make it less scientific. Lewin is known for his famous quote, "there is nothing so practical as a good theory."[274]

The Validity of Research is Questioned Because of the Collaborative Nature of the Researcher's Relationship with Clients in a Local Setting.

Many proponents of AR are challenging the traditional social science claim of neutrality and objectivity.[275] Participants are co-inquirers and contributors to the intervention's findings and solutions that foster lifelong learning to the researcher.

Viewed as Weak in the Procedure, Reporting of Results, and Reviewing

Technology made the accuracy of the interview possible. Interviews were recorded and transcribed through a paid software rev.ai. A copy was sent to each participant for validation to increase the research's credibility and trustworthiness.

Often Lacks Triangulation with Literature.

Triangulation is a method used to increase the validity and credibility of research findings. Credibility refers to trustworthiness, how believable a study is; validity refers to the accuracy of the idea being investigated when applied to another setting. In her study "The Point of Triangulation," Veronica Thurmond concluded that "the use of triangulation strategies does not strengthen a flawed study."[276] Researchers should use triangulation only if it contributes to the understanding of the phenomenon.

Generalization of the Findings

Contexts are the focus of AR and not general findings. The findings may accommodate more generalized findings, but it is not the immediate purpose of an AR.

---

[273] Gilbert, 240.
[274] Johnson and Christensen, 59.
[275] Gilbert, 239.
[276] Veronica A. Thurmond, "The Point of Triangulation," Journal of Nursing Scholarship 33, no. 3, accessed November 30, 2020, http://doi.wiley.com/10.1111/j.1547-5069.2001.00253.x.

APPENDIX 2

Interview Guide Approach by Patton in *Educational Research*,236.

This guide allows the interviewer (PAR) to ask specific open-ended questions with specific topics in mind. These topics and questions are provided and seen by the participants before the session. These questions are not in a particular order, and wordings can be changed at the time of the interview

Information about the interview:

Date and time of the Interview: _____
Context of the Participant: _____
Interview Session Length: between 40-90 minutes
Dissertation Title: "From the Philippines to the Global North: A Participatory Action Research on Intercultural Campus Ministry."

Casual Introduction:
Pray:
Purpose of this interview: My dissertation aims to inquire from your experiences as a Filipino missionary in your context. Your insights and contribution to this research will matter to the future Filipino missionaries who will serve in the Global North.

1. How did you start in the ministry? With Victory/Every Nation?
   a. Follow-up questions: How long have you been a full-time minister? Of the three-fold focus of Every Nation (Campus Ministry, Missions and Church Planting), majority of your time is devoted to_____? Was there a shift from before?

2. What led you to move to (local context)?
   a. Tell me more about that.
   b. Follow-up questions: How do you like it there? What are some cultural adjustments you/your family have to make? Is it easy to make friends? Tell me more about that.
3. When you think of your experiences of being a Filipino missionary in your context, what stands out in your mind? Tell me more about that, or elaborate further.
   a. Can you think of a specific situation and describe it to me?
4. What are some experiences of a Filipino missionary to the global north that is unique from being a missionary in the Philippines?
   a. What contexts and situations led to these experiences?
   b. Can you think of a specific situation and describe it to me

APPENDIX 3

Consent Form
From the Philippines to the Global North: A Participatory Action Research on Intercultural Campus Ministry.
You are being asked to take part in a research study on Filipino missionaries serving in the global north. From my conversation with Victory Philippines Missions' Director, your name was suggested as a potential candidate for this research. Note that this is not an institution-based project (by Victory nor Every Nation Ministries). Your participation will not affect your current or future ministry involvement. Please read this form carefully and ask any questions you may have before agreeing to take part in the study.

What the study is about:

The purpose of this study is to identify the challenges of Filipino missionaries serving in the global north and to engage them in diaspora missions in their local contexts through intercultural campus ministry. You must be a first-generation Filipino and work as a full-time staff or a spousal employee.

What we will ask you to do:

If you agree to be in this study, I will conduct an interview with you. You will see the interview questions before the session. The questions will be about your experiences as a Filipino missionary in your context. Each interview will be between 40-90 minutes, maximum of two interviews. The interview will be recorded and transcribed within three days. You will receive a copy of the transcription. During this time, you will validate your answers as well as omit or change when you think it was a misrepresentation of your answers. You might be included in the second interview for the intervention. You have an option to say no to the intervention.

Risks and benefits: I do not anticipate any risks to you participating in this study other than those encountered in day-to-day life. Your answers and your identity will be my highest priority. There are some benefits to you for participating in the study; a. opportunity to practice diaspora missions in your local contexts b. co-contributors to find solution to challenges (if any) c. pioneering something new

Compensation: No direct compensation to you.

Confidentiality: Your answers will be confidential. The records of this study will be kept private. In any sort of report, we make public we will not include any information that will make it possible to identify you. Research records will be kept in a locked file; only the researchers will have access to the records. If we tape-record the interview, we will destroy the tape after it has been transcribed, which we anticipate will be within two months of its taping.

Taking part is voluntary: Taking part in this study is completely voluntary. You may skip any questions that you do not want to answer. If you decide to take part in the study, you are free to withdraw at any time.

From the Philippines to the Global North: A Participatory Action Research on Intercultural Campus Ministry Consent Form.

If you have questions: The researcher conducting this study is Ria Llanto Martin. Please feel free to ask any questions that you have now. If you have questions following the study, you may contact Ria Llanto Martin at ria.martin@westernseminary.edu or call 1-206-251- 0439. If you have any questions or concerns regarding your rights as a subject in this study, you may contact the Institutional Review Board (IRB) chair.

You will be given a copy of this form to keep for your records.

Statement of Consent:

I have read the above information and have received answers to any questions I asked. I consent to take part in the study.

Your Signature _____
Date _____
Your Name (printed) _____
In addition to agreeing to participate, I also consent to having the interview tape-recorded.
Your Signature _____
Date _____
Your Name (printed) _____
Signature of person obtaining consent _____

Date _____Printed name of person obtaining consent _Ria Llanto Martin Date: March 22, 2021
This consent form will be kept by the researcher for at least three years beyond the end of the study.

APPENDIX 4

THEOLOGICAL COMPETENCY IN MISSIONS

Introduction

In chapter one, I mentioned that I will be adopting Diaspora Missions as my theoretical framework for this study. Relational realism coincides with Wan's diaspora missions. He defines relational missions as follows:

> Mission is a process by which Christians (individuals) and the Church (institutionally) continue on and carry out the *missio Dei* of the Triune God at both individual and institutional levels spiritually (saving souls) and socially (ushering in *shalom*) for redemption, reconciliation, and transformation; whereby missions is a way and means of accomplishing 'the mission' which was entrusted by the Triune God to the Church and Christians.[277]

The most common view of mission is a simplification of the Great Commission found in Matthew 28:16-20. While this is partly true, to essentialize the church's mission as going, teaching, and baptizing is to disregard the three years Jesus spent with his disciples. In other words, the commission is embedded in a plethora of contextual cues and common reference points like high context cultures. We ought to remind ourselves that Jesus lived with his disciples for three years before this popular mantra of missions came to be. The disciples were relationally connected to Jesus (vertical) while simultaneously going from village to village preaching the good news along with others (horizontally with *koinonia* and non-believers).

Missio Dei

What is God's purpose and mission in the world? One could start by considering Jesus' words to Peter:

> But who do you say that I am?" Simon Peter answered, "You are the Christ, the Son of the living God." And Jesus answered him, "You are blessed, Simon son of Jonah, because flesh and blood did not reveal this to you, but my Father in heaven! And I tell you that you are Peter, and on this rock, I will build my church, and the gates of Hades will not overpower it. I will give you the keys of the kingdom of heaven. Whatever you bind on earth will have been bound in heaven, and whatever you release on earth will have been released in heaven (Matt. 16:16-19, New English Translation).

---

[277] Wan et al., *Diaspora Missions to International Students*, 10.

When Jesus said, "I will build my church, and the gates of Hades will not overpower it," is a worthy hortatory point in expounding Christians' participation (continuation and carrying out) in missions. Jesus Christ is the one who initiated and established his church. I examine below two gospels, Mark and Luke, as the focus of this section for two reasons. Mark is the first gospel written after Jesus' death, while Matthew and Luke used Mark as the significant source of writing the Gospels.[278] Luke is paired with Acts, which the author referred to in his opening statement "In my former book, Theophilus, I wrote about all that Jesus began to do and teach" (Acts 1:1, New International Version). To present a significant understanding of missions, I chose the Gospels to see the first presentation of Jesus beginning his ministry, and the one most keyed in to the story as continued with the missional participation of his followers.

Part one of this chapter, *missio Dei*, is subdivided into three main topics: the theology of missions, Kingdom-oriented teachings, and the universality of the gospel's message and its approach to missions. These topics are extrapolations from Scriptures, shown on each table, the related texts from the Gospels of Mark and Luke that will further increase the heart of Filipino missionaries for missions. As Wan explains: "Historically, bearing witness to God was carried out by diasporic individuals/groups."[279] Examples may be found in Abraham who was called to live as a foreigner, the life of Joseph in Egypt, Daniel and his three friends in Babylon, and the scattered Christians during the exile.

One of the concerns brought about by the participants in the study is not only the lack of mentoring but also training in theology. I propose these foundational concepts to strengthen their understanding of missions on diaspora missiology and the relationality of Jesus' ministry. Continuing their study in theology through a seminary is highly encouraged.

Foundational Concepts

Theology of Missions

Missions Began in the Old Testament, and the Opening Remarks from Both Mark and Luke are Testaments to the "Good News" that Jesus is the Messianic King Referred to in the OT.[280]

---

[278] Macgregor, K. R. (2016). Mark, Gospel Of. In J. D. Barry, D. Bomar, D. R. Brown, R. Klippenstein, D. Mangum, C. Sinclair Wolcott, ... W. Widder (Eds.), *The Lexham Bible Dictionary*. Bellingham, Wa: Lexham Press. On Markan Priority, and Luke's Use of Mark, See Goodacre, Mark, *The Case Against Q: Studies In Markan Priority and The Synoptic Problem* (Harrisburg, Pa: Trinity Press International, 2002).

[279] Wan, *Diaspora Missions to International Students*, 14.

[280] The New International Version is the translation unless otherwise noted.

Table 7 Jesus is the Messianic King

Mark	Luke
1:1-2 The beginning of the good news about Jesus the Messiah, the Son of God, as it is written in Isaiah the prophet. "I will send my messenger ahead of you, who will prepare your way a voice of one calling in the wilderness, 'Prepare the way for the Lord, make straight paths for him.'	1:1-4 Many have undertaken to draw up an account of the things that have been fulfilled among us, just as they were handed down to us by those who from the first were eyewitnesses and servants of the word. 3 With this in mind since I myself have carefully investigated everything from the beginning, I too decided to write an orderly account for you, most excellent Theophilus, so that you may know the certainty of the things you have been taught. 1:26-33, 35 the birth of Jesus foretold to Mary "the Holy One to be born, will be called the Son of God." 2:11 the Birth of Jesus and the angel's appearance to the shepherds that a "savior has been born, he is the Messiah the Lord."

Both texts are confirmations that Jesus is the fulfillment of the prophecies referred to by Isaiah in Isa 40 and 61 (as well as Malachi, which Mark has combined with Isaiah). Missions is a Trinitarian mission = *missio Dei.* See the diagram below to illustrate *missio Dei, the* pattern of intra-trinitarian relationships from Isaiah forty alone.

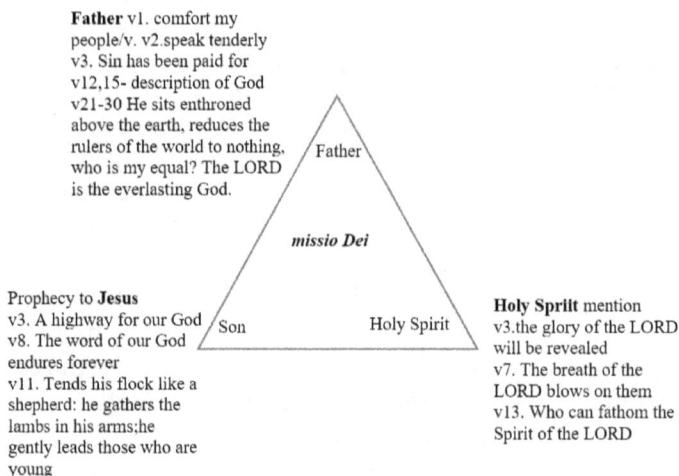

Father v1. comfort my
people/v. v2.speak tenderly
v3. Sin has been paid for
v12,15- description of God
v21-30 He sits enthroned
above the earth, reduces the
rulers of the world to nothing,
who is my equal? The LORD
is the everlasting God.

Father

missio Dei

Son   Holy Spirit

Prophecy to **Jesus**
v3. A highway for our God
v8. The word of our God
endures forever
v11. Tends his flock like a
shepherd: he gathers the
lambs in his arms;he
gently leads those who are
young

Holy Sprilt mention
v3.the glory of the LORD
will be revealed
v7. The breath of the
LORD blows on them
v13. Who can fathom the
Spirit of the LORD

Figure 20 *Missio Dei* from Isaiah 40

John the Baptist prepared the way for the One who is to come, to prepare the way of the Lord and to the One who will come after him, who is more powerful than he (Mark 1:4-8). Luke's reference to Isaiah 60, which, after reading the scroll in the synagogue, Jesus declares that he is the fulfillment of that prophecy. This messianic prophecy was confirmed by Jesus after his resurrection to his disciples in the last chapter of Luke, saying that "This is what I told you while I was still with you: Everything must be fulfilled that is written about me in the Law of Moses, the Prophets and the Psalms" (Luke 24:44, New International Version).

Two pivotal characters from Luke are Simeon (2:26-32) and Anna, the prophetess (2:36-38), who, in their old age, affirmed seeing the Messiah— referring to Jesus before their passing. Anna's exact words upon seeing Jesus as "the redemption of Israel." It is noteworthy that Anna belonged to the tribe Asher, a tribe that was part of the ten who spread fear among Israelites when Moses sent twelve spies from each tribe to scout the land. The only two tribes spared were those of Joshua and Caleb. These two tribes entered the promised land in faith, while the rest of the tribes remained fearful: "the tribe joined the rest of Israel in rejecting the optimistic reports of Caleb and Joshua about the land of Canaan (Num 13:30–14:10).[281] Nevertheless, the beginning of Luke represented a tribe that was lost and now redeemed and included in the story of God's faithfulness.

---

[281] Elwell, W. A., & Beitzel, B. J. (1988). Asher, Tribe of. In *Baker Encyclopedia Of The Bible* (Vol. 1, P. 212). Grand Rapids, MI: Baker Book House.

Jesus Began his Ministry with the Father and the Holy Spirit. Jesus' Mission is the Mission of the Triune God. His Mission is to Proclaim the Good News, Proclaim Freedom, and Proclaim the Year of the Lord's Favor.

Table 8 The Mission is the Mission of the Triune God

Mark	Luke

1:1-8 John the Baptist, who was called to prepare the way for the Lord, began:
I will send my messenger ahead of you,
    who will prepare your way" b—
   3 "a voice of one calling in the wilderness,
    'Prepare the way for the Lord,
      make straight paths for him.
John was tasked to prepare the way of the Lord by preaching a baptism of repentance for the forgiveness of sins to people from the whole Judean countryside and all of Jerusalem. The people responded as they confessed their sins. One more powerful than John will come, the One will baptize with the Holy Spirit.
1:10-11 baptism of Jesus
1:14-15 Jesus' opening work is the proclamation of the Gospel of God, the announcement of the arrival of the Kingdom of God, and the call to repentance and believe the good news.
1:28 His mere presence created conflict among the demonic spirits that caught the people saying, "What is this? A new teaching with authority! He even commands the unclean spirits, and they obey him."
Jesus heals many (physical illnesses and demonic spirits 1:29-34, 1:40-45, 2:1-5, 3:11, 8:22,9:14-29, 14:1-8
With this new teaching with authority - Jesus publicly declares the forgiveness of their sins and empowering peoples' faith upon healing -Jesus' authority to forgive sins 2:5,8, 2:5-12 (with forgiveness of sins), 3:28 (forgiveness of sins) 5:34,36, 10:52, 11:22-25.
	4:14-19 (Messianic mission from Isa 61): The Spirit of the Lord is on me because he has anointed me to proclaim good news to the poor. He has sent me to proclaim freedom for the prisoners and recovery of sight for the blind, to set the oppressed free, to proclaim the year of the Lord's favor and the day of vengeance of our God. The fulfillment of the prophecy from Isa 61: Jesus heals many (4:40, 5:12, 7:21, 9:11, 13:31, 17:11-17, 18:42 including raising dead people back to life 7:11-17
	Demons came out of many (4:41, 7:21, 8:26-39, 9:37-43, 11:14, 13:10
	-Proclamation of the Good News of the Kingdom of God to other towns also, because that is why I was sent 4:43, 8:1, 9:11
	Jesus' teaching on every village of Galilee, Judea, Jerusalem 10:1 and when he was rejected in Samaritan village, he went to the next 9:55

The ministry that Jesus began involves the Father and the Holy Spirit. It is crucial to understand that even Jesus, the Son of God, did not operate individually. His whole ministry involves the Father and the Holy Spirit, as depicted in Jesus' baptism. *The mission of Jesus is the mission of the Triune God.*

Christopher Wright affirms, "Mission is not ours, mission is God's. Certainly, the mission of God is the prior reality of which flows any mission that we get involved in."[282] Barth and Hartenstein connected the mission with the doctrine of the trinity, highlighting the intra-trinitarian movement of God himself over history:

> So the phrase originally meant 'the sending of God' –in the sense of the Father sending of the Son and their sending of the Holy Spirit. All human mission, in this perspective, is seen as a participation in and extension of this divine sending.[283]

Furthermore, Bosch defines *missio Dei* as:

> God's self-revelation as the One who loves the world, God's involvement in and with the world, the nature and activity of God, which embraces both the church and the world, in which the church is privileged to participate. *Missio Dei* enunciates the good news that God is a God-for-people.[284]

Wan pointed out the key element in mission is the pattern of sending and submission as interaction within the triune God. He quotes Gibson, who claims that the foundation of mission begins in the Triune God and what unfolds in the history of redemption is the covenant of redemption between the Persons of the Trinity. "Mission did not begin in history with Eve, Abraham, or Israel. Theologically, 'mission' is *missio Dei* intra-Trinity."[285] Leithart's remarks I mentioned in chapter two bear repeating:

> But the saving message of the gospel needs to be heard and believed, and God doesn't delegate the task of making sure that the Word is heard and believed to some subordinate. Of course, human beings proclaim the gospel, human beings evangelize; but it's the Spirit of God who ensures that the message has power unto salvation. It's the Spirit of God that ensures that those who hear the message believe the message. It's not simply that the Father sent the Son, and then human beings proclaimed the good news of the Son. God Himself takes on the task, *not only of saving us but also of ensuring that that saving message is heard and believed (emphasis mine)* so

---

282 Christopher J. H. Wright, *The Mission of God*, 62.
283 Christopher J. H. Wright, *The Mission of God*, 62
284 David J. Bosch, *Transforming Mission: Paradigm Shifts in Theology of Mission*, 20th Anniversary edition. (Maryknoll, N.Y: Orbis, 2011), 4.
285 Wan, *Diaspora Missions to International Students*, 15.

that all the nations might know that Jesus Christ is Lord and all of them might bow their knee to Him.[286]

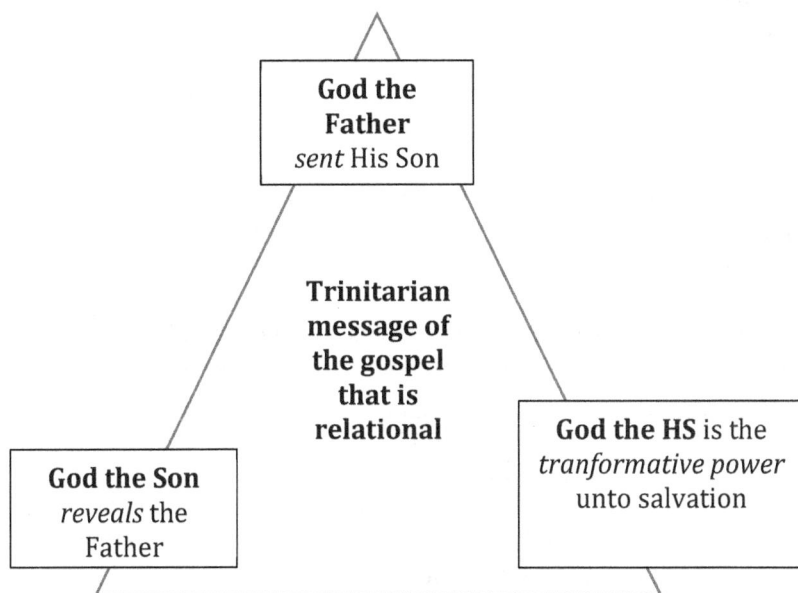

Figure 21 Trinitarian Message of the Gospel

Isa 60 talked about three kinds of proclamation that encapsulate Jesus' ministry: the proclamation of good news, the proclamation of freedom, and the proclamation of the year of the Lord's favor. The word "proclaim" in Hebrew and Greek means "to call," "to make known," or "to announce good tidings or good news." In Greek, it is frequently associated with preaching. The proclamation is an announcement worthy of being heard; it is a matter of truth, without solicitation from the opinions of the majority. In Jesus' ministry, he did not only proclaim, *but he is the embodied good news, freedom, and year of the Lord's favor.* Furthermore, proclamation involves moving from one place to the next, one village to the next, and nearby villages: "Let us go somewhere else—to the nearby villages—so I can preach there also, that is why I have come" (Mark 1:38-39, New International Version). It is an early depiction of the polycentric nature of Jesus' ministry.

The opening verse for the book of Mark points that Jesus, the Messiah, is the beginning of good news. Angels appeared to Mary, saying that she is to name the baby Jesus—Yeshua "YHWH is salvation or YHWH saves/has saved,"[287]an allusion to the divinity and salvific efficacy of the Christ. Jesus' opening work is the proclamation of the gospel of God, the announcement of the arrival of the

---

[286] Peter J. Leithart, *TH215 Trinitarian Theology.*

[287] Ben F. Meyer, "Jesus (Person): Jesus Christ," Ed. David Noel Freedman, *The Anchor Yale Bible Dictionary* (New York: Doubleday, 1992), 773.

Kingdom of God, and the call to repentance and belief in the good news (1:14-15). His presence shook the underworld as they acknowledged his lordship both in the natural and supernatural world. The people realized by responding, "What is this? A new teaching with authority! He even commands the unclean spirits, and they obey him. So, the news about him spread quickly throughout all the region around Galilee." To proclaim the year of the Lord's favor is to proclaim of the lordship of Christ, who has authority over demonic forces, to forgive sins and heal many sicknesses and diseases.

Jesus is the Author of Missions, and his Invitation to his People is the Answer to a Plentiful Harvest and Few Workers. The Help for the Plentiful Harvest will Come from the Redeemed Ones.

Table 9 The Extension of Jesus' Ministry from the Twelve to Others

Mark	Luke
Called those he wanted and appointed the twelve to preach and have authority 3:13-18, 6:6b-13	Jesus invitation to his mission: 5:1-11 First to the twelve, 8: 1-3 Extended to some women who have been cured of evil spirits and diseases like Mary, Joanna, Susanna, and many others 10:1-4 Adding seventy more for the harvest is plentiful, and the workers are few

Even though John the Baptist's ministry chronologically began before Jesus, his calling is not divorced or separated from Jesus' ministry. The calling of the twelve and the gradual increasing involvement of "some other women" to the additional seventy others is both missional and ecclesiological. Luke mentioned that there were "women who joined, along with many others, were those who have been cured of diseases and healed" (8:1-3). The disciples' involvement with Jesus' mission is the ecclesiological purpose, and the ecclesiological purpose supports the mission. Jesus' invitation to his mission is to account for and solve the problem of the harvest being plentiful and the workers being few. The purpose of the church is not detached from his mission, and his mission is not detached from his church either. Jesus did it relationally. At this point, the integration between ecclesiology and missiology is self-evident. The diagram below demonstrates the vertical and horizontal relationships (relational realism paradigm) when Jesus inaugurated his missions on earth.

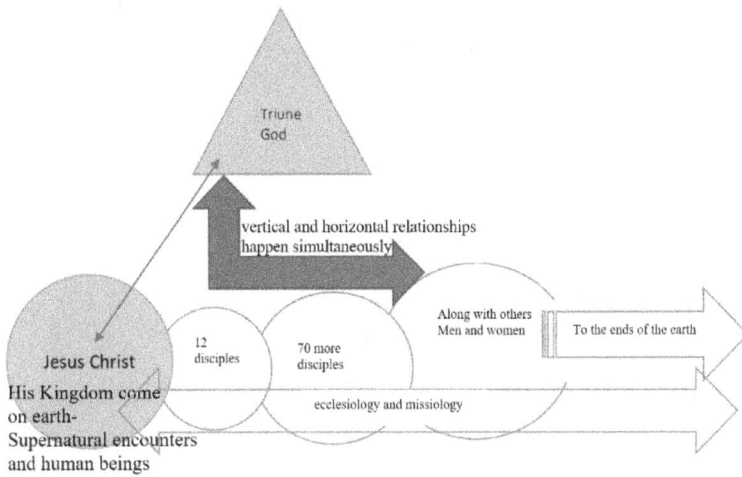

Figure 22 Jesus as the Author of Missions

Kingdom Orientation (Jesus' Counter-Cultural Teachings)

The Kingdom of God Requires a Change of Allegiance from the Worldly Paradigm to a God-Centered, Eternity-Based Orientation.

Table 10 His Kingdom Culture

Mark	Luke
The Son of man is the Lord of the Sabbath 2:27 Parable of the Sower 4:1-20 The kingdom of God is like the growing seed 4:26, mustard seed 4:30-34, come as like the little children 10:14-16 Forfeit one's soul and gain the whole world 8:38 Cost of being disciple 8:34-35 Divorce and adultery 10:2-12 What's impossible with man is possible with God 10:27 The greatest commandment 12:28-34	Love your enemies/ lend without expecting anything in return (6:27-36 Do not judge others (6:37-41 No good tree bears bad fruit (6:43-46) Wise builders (6:46 Parables (Sower 8:5-15 My mother and brothers are those who hear God's word and put it into practice 8:21 Rejoice that your names are written in heaven (10:20 Love your neighbor (show mercy 10:25-37 Choose wisely...the one that is needed 10:38-42 on Mary and Martha Life does not consist in an abundance of possessions – the parable of the Rich Fool 12:14 Life is more than food, and body and more than clothes 12:22 Repentance or perish, forgiveness (how far is this from the story?) 13:1-8, 17: 1-6 The Kingdom of God is like a mustard seed and the yeast 12:18-20 Those who exalt themselves will be humbled, and those who humbled themselves will be exalted Parable of the Banquet 12:13-23, 18:9-15 (parable of the pharisee and the tax collector Welcome sinners and eat with them- Parable of the lost sheep 15:1-7 Reconciliation of families with the radical story of the lost son 15:11-32 Use worldly wealth to gain friends for yourselves so that you will be welcomed into eternal dwellings. You cannot serve both money and God 16:9 Anyone who divorces his wife and marries another woman commits adultery, and the man who marries a divorced woman commits adultery 16:18 Whoever tries to save their lives will lose it 17:33 Do not hinder the little children from coming into the kingdom of God 18:15-17 Who then can be saved? What is impossible with man is possible with God. 18:27 No one who has left home or wife or brothers or sisters for the kingdom of God will fail to receive many times as much in this age, and in the age to come eternal life 18:29-30.

Missionaries as partners of Jesus in his mission to the world should look for opportunities to listen and obey the Holy Spirit's leading concerning prevailing cultures and influences in their context irreconcilable with Jesus's teachings.

To become a follower of Christ is the opposite treatment Pharisees received in society. There is no room for self-aggrandizement, titular privileges, nor worldly comfort in becoming a follower of Christ. No "Man of God" syndrome, as Murrell describes in the previous chapter. To follow Christ is to deny oneself—any inclinations that would draw attention to oneself. To take up the cross is not just the hardships and the persecutions in following Christ, but the unpopularity, shamefulness, and mockery that the society associates with it. The answer to saving one's soul is the forfeiture of worldly matters.

A word on soteriology: the good news is available for all, from educated and privileged Pharisees to outcasts, marginalized sinners, including children ("let the little children come"). Salvation—that which is impossible for a man—God has made possible. So that the *righteousness that God requireth is also the one he provideth.*

Faith is Belief Expressed in Action. Faith is a Desideratum for the Forgiveness of Sins and the Force Behind Forgiving Others. Healing and Forgiveness Expressed by Faith are Commendable to Jesus.

Table 11 Healing and Forgiveness is Part of Jesus' Ministry

Mark	Luke
2:1-2 Healing and forgiving the paralytic "When Jesus saw their faith, Son your sins are forgiven." 5:21-34 "Daughter, your faith has made you well." 10:46-52 Healing of Bartimaeus "your faith has healed you."	7:36-50 woman with an alabaster jar "then Jesus said to her your sins are forgiven." 5:17-26 healing and forgiving the paralytic "when Jesus saw their faith, he said, Friend, your sins are forgiven." 7:1-6 Centurion's faith "I have not found such great faith even in Israel." 17:1-6 it only takes faith the size of a mustard seed to forgive others 8:48- Syrophoenician Woman's daughter "Daughter, your faith has made you well." 17:19 the grateful leper "your faith has made you well." 18:35-42 Healing a blind man "your faith has healed you."

Faith described in both Mark and Luke's accounts requires action. The healing of a paralytic man required an action from his four friends to lower him down on a mat to receive healing from Jesus. The woman with an alabaster jar began to weep at Jesus' feet, wiped her tears with her hair, and poured perfume on his feet. A centurion's faith that Jesus commended, "I have not found such great faith, even in Israel," was sent for Jesus twice, first from the centurion's

Jewish leaders and the second time by his friends. The centurion did not even believe it necessary for Jesus to come in person—in his words: "say the word, and my servant will be healed." Faith's role in the healing and forgiveness of sins is commendable to Jesus. The indissoluble combination of faith and healing on five accounts from Luke that Jesus paused and highlighted in the story is noteworthy.

The Universality of the Gospel

The Gospel Transcends Human and Spiritual Barriers, Socio-Economic Strata, as well as Different Schools of Thought – Pharisees, Sadducees and Herodias, any Political Affiliation (E.G., The Centurion), Religious Or Non-Religious, Physically and Spiritually Oppressed.

Table 12 The Universality of the Gospel

Mark	Luke
2:13 Eats with Levi from Alphaeus a tax collector 3:10 Large crowd followed from Galilee, and many people come from Judea, Jerusalem, Idumea, and the regions across the Jordan and around Tyre and Sidon 5:21-43 Jairus, one of the synagogue leaders and a woman bleeding for 12 years 7:24 Healed the daughter of the woman who was Syrophoenician. 11:17 house of prayer for all nations 12:41-44- poor widow's offering 12:13, 18 Conversation with Pharisees and Herodians 12:13 and Sadducees 13:10 And the Gospel must first be preached to all nations 15:21A certain man from Cyrene, Simon the Father of Alexander and Rufus 15:38 Centurion who exclaimed "surely this man was the Son of God" after Jesus' death 15:38 15:42-43 Joseph of Arimathea- a prominent member, took Jesus' dead body 16:1-8 Mary Magdalene, Mary mother of James and Salome, witnessed Jesus' resurrected body 13:10 "for the Gospel must be first preached to all nations.	2:29-32 "Sovereign Lord, as you have promised, you may now dismiss your servant in peace. For my eyes have seen your salvation, which you have prepared in the sight of all nations: a light for revelation to the Gentiles, and the glory of your people Israel. 5:27 Jesus went out and ate with Levi the tax collector, a wealthy tax collector 4:24-30 when there was a famine in the land, Elijah was sent to a widow in Zarephath in the region of Sidon and Naaman the Syrian- both foreigners 7:1-9 Centurion faith healed his servant "I tell you, I have not found such great faith even in Israel" 7:36-50 Jesus had dinner with a Pharisee while interacting with the woman of Alabaster jar 8:40-56 Jairus, a synagogue leader and a woman who had been subject to bleeding for twelve years, touched the edge of his cloak 13:29 "People will come from east and west, north and south, and will take their places at the feast in the kingdom of God 17:11- 19 Jesus healed all ten, but only the foreigner returned to Praise God. 14:1-4 One Sabbath Jesus went to eat in the house of a prominent Pharisee and in front of him was a man suffering from abnormal swelling of his body- Jesus healed him 19:1-10 The twelve were with Jesus as well as some women who had been cured of evil spirits and diseases like Mary, Joanna, Susanna and many other women 21:1-4 poor widow's offering 23:26- 43 universality of the Gospel ended not just the inclusion of Centurion's confession of Jesus as the Son of God from the book of Mark, but Jesus forgave "them" centurions and onlookers for they do not know what they are doing and Jesus's response to the criminal "Today, you will be with me in paradise." 24:47 "repentance for the forgiveness of sins will be preached in his name to all nations, beginning at Jerusalem."

These are overwhelming pieces of evidence from both Gospel accounts about the universality of the gospel's message. The universality of the gospel begins at Jesus' "unintentional" first ministry at the temple with Joseph and Mary. There, an older man named Simeon witnessed to have seen Jesus as salvation—a Messiah to all peoples extending to Gentiles as confirmed in the following texts, Luke 2:29-32.

Throughout Jesus' ministry, he ministered to all kinds of people; both rich and poor (from Levi the wealthy tax collector to the widow from Zarepath), educated and uneducated (to both Pharisees and fishermen), prominent and nameless (from Jairus, a synagogue ruler to a nameless woman bleeding for twelve years), including men and women. Most of the participants in this research have expressed questions like, "What is good news for the rich?" or, "How do you share the good news to a wealthy nation if you come from a place of poverty?" In Jesus' example, the message of the gospel *is* good news for all peoples. His lordship and salvation power relies on his deity as God, not based on how he fulfills the need. By definition, our participation in the mission is relational in all aspects. If we limit the preaching of the gospel as per need basis, we reduce the message to consumerism, a managerial business approach.[288]

And yet we still face these questions today when considering practical implications of the gospel's universality. Needs-based managerial missiology begs the question, "What is good news for the rich?," because they *seem* to have everything. They seem to already lack nothing. However, *missio Dei* is first relational: John 17 testifies, "For you granted him (Jesus) authority over all people that he might give eternal life to all those you have given him. Now, this is eternal life: that they know you, the only true God, and Jesus Christ whom you have sent" (John 17:2-3, New International Version). *Missio Dei* is relational in essence and its approach. Where is God leading you, and who is God leading into your lives? It is a partnership. Are they wealthy? Are they poor? Did he/she come from a place you have never been before? Diaspora missiology and relational realism do not classify ministry based on need nor status. Rich people can participate in the mission of God, like Lydia in Acts 16, as much as the poor widower who gave her all in the Gospel of Mark.

At times, Jesus' encounters with the Jews were scandalous to the elites and privileged "chosen" people. His teachings and his association with outcasts, sinners, and foreigners countercultural that Jesus' intention and salvation message is salvation for all. At one point, Jesus reiterated this in Luke 8:21, "my mother and my brother are those who hear God's word and put them into practice" (NET). Here, the family was extended from bloodline to Christ's blood for all and those who hear and put God's word into practice.

Jesus singled out the centurion's faith for his servant's healing in Luke 7 when he said: "I have not found such *great faith* even in Israel," (emphasis

---

[288] For a full review and critique on Managerial Missiology, check chapter seven of, Enoch Wan, *Diaspora Missiology: Theory, Methodology, and Practice* 2nd ed (Portland, OR: Institute of Diaspora Studies-USA, 2011), pp. 111-121.

mine) commending a faith of a foreigner throughout Israel. Furthermore, the gospel did not fail to mention an intrusion from Simon, the Father of Alexander and Rufus, who helped Jesus carry the cross along the way. The author provided enough details for a reader to be curious and explore the odd insertion. Simon of Cyrene, a region in North Africa, today's Libya,[289] was not a local Jew, but a man of African origin. This particular man was part of the crucifixion story, a foreigner invited to carry the cross.

At the time of Jesus' death, Luke assiduously narrated the final picture, the denouement of the universality of the gospel, with Jesus' last breath, his disciples, onlookers, centurion guards, and criminals on each side witnessing this crucial moment. Jesus was offering forgiveness to the onlookers who "do not know what they are doing," and his response to the criminal's confession: "Today, you will be with me in paradise." Right after Jesus' death, the first confession of his kingship was uttered by a Roman centurion, "Surely this was the Son of God."

Joseph of Arimathea asked for Jesus' body, a member of Sanhedrin. Sanhedrin is "the highest legislative body in Jewish Palestine, the supreme judicial court, the grand jury for important cases, the council of the Pharisaic school, and the final court of appeals in deciding *halakic* questions."[290] His gesture was opposite to Pharisaic remarks and behavior throughout the Gospels. This is yet another illustration of the universality of the gospel, impacting a prominent and wealthy leader in the society.

Acts, a Continuation of Jesus' Ministry

The rationale of referencing Luke was from the opening verse of Acts "In my former book, Theophilus, I wrote about all that Jesus began to do and to teach." Filled with powerful stories regarding continuing Jesus' ministry from the Gospels, the book of Acts is loaded with stories, struggles, victories, and the death of martyrs yet unraveling the dynamism, polycentric and multidirectional nature of a church founded by Jesus. In many places, Scripture asserts the universality of the gospel, the intercultural nature of Jesus' ministry in the Gospels, the mission of God from OT to NT, and in Revelation, how Christ's church will consist of "every nation, tribe, people and language, standing before the throne and before the Lamb dressed in long white robes, and with palm branches in their hands" (Rev 7:9, New English Translation). It has become apparent that engaging in missions initially to people of the same tribe has become the default and a convenient option in missions, especially to diverse cities. This section displayed Jesus' ministry that proved otherwise.

---

[289] John Piper, "What's the Significance of Simon Carrying Jesus's Cross?" Desiring God. Last modified April 19, 2019, accessed April 8, 2020, https://www.desiringgod.org/interviews/whats-the-significance-of-simon-carrying-jesuss-cross.

[290] Saldarini, A. J. (1992). Sanhedrin. in D. N. Freedman (Ed.), *The Anchor Yale Bible Dictionary* (Vol. 5, P. 975). New York: Doubleday.

The book of Acts is a popular reference concerning missions and church planting. However, Jesus is the master-builder of his church who will partner with him in missions. "Many students of church planting begin their study in the book of Acts because the apostles were sent out and empowered by the Holy Spirit to make disciples...There may be theological reasons for this, but starting with Paul's ministry has certain disadvantages."[291] This shows that the later ministry to the Gentiles depicts that the universality of the gospel are mere continuations of how Jesus modeled a polycentric approach to missions. Here are two common biblical references about Peter and Paul's ministry to the gentiles.

Peter and Cornelius

In this story, an angel appeared to Cornelius to send someone for Peter while the Holy Spirit spoke to Peter through a vision to go with the man that would take him to Cornelius. As described in Acts 10, Cornelius was a devout, God-fearing man and prayed to God generously. He was a follower who gives to those in need, regularly prays to God, and operates in the prophetic gift, "Now we are here in the presence of God to listen to everything the Lord has commanded you to tell us" (Acts 10:33, New English Translation).

There was an established relationship between Cornelius and God before his appointment with Peter. Peter responded, "I now realize how true it is that God does not show favoritism but accepts from every nation the one who fears him and does what is right." It was a realization for Peter and the people with him. It was not the starting point of the ministry to the Gentiles. Instead, Peter's response, "I *now* realize," (emphasis added) is a confirmation that God started the ministry to the Gentiles during Jesus' time.

Along with others (circumcised believers), Peter's cultural lens hindered him from seeing this ministry that led to the council of Jerusalem in Acts 15. It was not the first recorded Gentile conversation, as some scholars have claimed. Cornelius the centurion in Acts may be the first in Acts but not in Luke's writings as a whole, for the one who said, "Surely this is the Son of God!" at the crucifixion of Jesus was a Roman centurion as well.

Ananias and Saul

Another point of clarification is Paul's appointment to the Gentiles. In Acts 9:15-16, "But the Lord said to Ananias, 'Go! This man is my chosen instrument to proclaim my name to the Gentiles and their kings and the people of Israel. I will show him how much he must suffer for my name.'" One might also translate "to proclaim my name" as "to carry my name." A key point to consider is the appointment given to Paul to carry the name of Jesus to the Gentiles. The

---

[291] Craig Ott and Gene Wilson, *Global Church Planting: Biblical Principles and Best Practices for Multiplications* (Grand Rapids, MI: Baker Academics, 2011), 39.

phrase "carry my name" signified continuity rather than a brand new start of what is bound to happen.

In this section, I presented how one's understanding of missions is a participation of what Jesus already initiated during his ministry from the gospels. For first-generation Filipino missionaries in the global north, ministering to the wealthy is part of the universal message of the Good News. One must move away from needs-based missions to Holy Spirit empowered message of the gospel, salvation including the wealthy. To know God is eternal life. He offers a relationship with Him, more than comfort in this troubling world. Another highlight I want to point out is the polycentric nature of Jesus' ministry. He ministered to people from all walks of life, different religious backgrounds, people groups, and status such that in Acts, churches were happening in different parts simultaneously that enabled Paul to minister as an apostle. Christians from different cities welcomed him, provided food and a place to stay. A scriptural understanding of mission is essential for missions. First-generation Filipino missionaries in the global north must understand that Jesus modeled a polycentric approach to mission regardless of their background.

The second part of this chapter is on the concept of *imago Dei*, how one's understanding of the Triune God affects a missionary individually (first vertically) and institutionally (secondly horizontal), ushering in shalom for redemption, reconciliation, and transformation.

APPENDIX 5

THE INTERVENTION

Introduction

Intervention is the "act" in the methodological process explained in chapter three. This part of the process is a collaboration between the participants and researcher where the goal is to engage Filipino missionaries in diaspora missions through an intercultural campus ministry. However, after reflecting on the participants' answers, the restraining forces identified in chapter three took precedence before engaging them in diaspora missions. In the process, the intervention became a two-part series, decrease the restraining forces through intercultural competency and increase the driving force in missions. This two-part intervention will ultimately lead to diaspora missions involvement through intercultural campus ministry

Jane Vella, author of *Learning to Listen Learning to Teach: The Power of Dialogue in Educating Adults*, whose forty years of teaching experiences in Africa, Asia, and North America, concluded, "adults learn best through a dialogue" that takes place in an atmosphere of "mutual respect and safety, and with learning designs that are grounded in the reality of their lives."[292] She made significant contributions to adult education, particularly dialogue education.[293] In her book, she describes seven sequential questions for learning. In this section, I will address each of these questions.

Who?

The participants for this intervention are the first-generation Filipino missionaries who participated in this research. Seven participants responded agreeably out of the initial list of ten. During the interview, it became apparent that the participants shared a similar background before moving to the global north.

a) They all have a positive Christian background, worshipful experience, powerful preaching, and a welcoming community.
b) They witnessed the involvement of the young generation in missions and church planting.
c) It is in the community that they experienced relational discipleship.

---

[292] "Dr. Jane Vella," Global Learning Partners, accessed May 7, 2021, https://www.globallearningpartners.com/the-team/jane-vella/.

[293] "Her teaching and work have inspired a generation of educators, community developers, and health workers. Some of their experiences with Dialogue Education are outlined in the book *Dialogue Education at Work: Case Studies* (October 2003). "Dr. Jane Vella," Global Learning Partners, https://www.globallearningpartners.com/the-team/jane-vella/.

d) They all have a wealth of ministry experience in the Philippines (for at least ten years before moving abroad).

e) None of them received intercultural competency training specific to their context. This intercultural competency training is needed to work with a diverse team and in evangelism and discipleship.

f) The majority have expressed that mentoring structure is needed to thrive in their context.

g) Calling to nations and responding to that calling is vital as a Christ-follower.

h) All participants have a good foundation of their identity with God.

i) All participants (except one) are part of an existing leadership team.

j) All participants acknowledged that their city is diverse and saw the opportunity to reach nations within their city with international students and immigrant families.

Why?

Based on the findings, lack of intercultural competency in evangelism and discipleship and ongoing peer mentorship, a dialogical platform in which they can bounce ideas, will decrease the restraining forces in their current situation. The specific need for intercultural competency are:

a.) Trust and relationship building

b.) Understanding the rhythms of life in their context

c.) Value of time

d.) Intercultural communication within the leadership setting

e.) Theology in their context

This intervention will provide the dialogical platform integrating relational realism in the methodology to present and discuss the intercultural challenges in their context. Even though the participants adhere to their identity as Filipino to be an advantage in missions, the above concerns are restraining them from reaching the nations within their city. As I reflect on these findings, addressing these challenges will lead to engaging in intercultural campus ministry. Providing a dialogical platform regarding these challenges will decrease the restraining forces that prevent first-generation Filipino missionaries from fully thriving and reaching the nations within their city through an intercultural campus ministry.

When and Where?

A few weeks after the individual interviews, the first intervention took place. It was received well, expressing the need for another follow-up. One response, "I am learning a lot," came from a Filipino missionary who has been serving in the global north for almost three decades. The solution was to propose an informal peer mentoring group meeting once a month where the researcher would present one intercultural challenge per meeting and have a discussion time. The proposal is informal because this research is not institutionally based. The participants are free to attend or not to any of the future interventions. The proposed informal intervention, or what is now called peer mentoring, would take place once a month, tackling one intercultural challenge at a time, as an hour and a half at a time through online video calls.

What?

According to Jane Vella, this question answers the immediate needs of field staff. This question provides the skills, knowledge, and attitudes. For this context, each peer mentoring session will have these components: Attitudes, Skills, and Theology.

Attitudes

The first twenty minutes of the session is an icebreaker or activity that will facilitate:
   a) Cultural sensitivity: awareness of one's own cultural assumptions.
   b) Cultural empathy: awareness of others' cultural assumptions.
   c) Cultural humility: managing the tension between both assumptions.

Skills

I reserve thirty to forty minutes to present and discuss one intercultural challenge presented in chapter five. Four intercultural conflicts emerged based on the interview, contexts (high and low context), time orientation, trust formation, degree of interdependence (individualistic and collectivist cultures). Some of the questions raised during the interview were:
   a) Time: How to share life with a community that has no time for new friends?
   b) Trust: How do you build trust in a community that does not have time?
   c) Relationship: How do you build a relationship when there is no trust?
   d) Community engagement: How do you build a community to an individualistic or independent culture?

Theology

The purpose of this section is to increase the driving force by sharing Scriptures from chapter six on *missio Dei* and *imago Dei.*

What for?

These are the desired learning objectives for the intervention:
  a) Increase cultural sensitivity through self-awareness of one's cultural assumptions.
  b) Identify cultural assumptions Filipino missionaries bring into their understanding and approach to missions.
  c) Increase cultural empathy through awareness of other peoples' cultural assumptions.
  d) View intercultural conflicts as solvable gaps through intercultural competency.
  e) Practice cultural humility when intercultural conflict arises.
  f) Find mentorship within the peer mentoring group where they can process their conflict and find solutions.
  g) Move from a monocultural paradigm toward an intercultural paradigm in their missions engagement.
  h) Expand their passion for the campus and missions through intercultural campus ministry involvement.
  i) Demonstrate that intercultural campus ministry is a Scriptural way of participating in diaspora missions.
  j) Reignite the need to reach the next generation more than ever.
  k) Cultivate relationality in Christian practice and missions.

How?

Relational Pedagogy

   This step models the dialogue approach without diminishing the importance of relationships. Vella shared twelve principles of dialogue education, and one of the principles is sound relationships.[294] This section examines the relationship between the instructor/facilitator and the learner. Vella states: "friendship but no dependency, fun without trivializing learning, dialogue between adult men and women who feel themselves, peers."[295] She quotes Margaret Wheatley, whose expertise range from organizational behavior, chaos theory, and living systems science,

   In quantum world, relationship is the key determiner of everything. Subatomic particles come into form and are observed only as they are in relationship to something else. They do not exist as independent 'things.' Quantum physics paints a strange yet enticing view of a world that, as

---

[294] The twelve principles from Jane Vella's *Learning to Listen, Learning to Teach* are Needs assessment, Safety, Sound relationships, Sequence of content and reinforcement, Praxis-action with reflection, Respect for learners as decision makers.
[295] Jane Vella, *Learning to Listen, Learning to Teach: The Power of Dialogue in Educating Adults* (San Francisco ,CA :Jossey-Bass, 2002), 85-100.

Heisenberg describes it, 'it appears as a complicated tissue of events in which connections of different kinds alternate or overlap or combine and thereby determine the texture of the whole'. These unseen connections between what were previously thought to be separate entities are the fundamental ingredient of all creation.[296]

Sound learning for learning, according to Vella, involves "respect, safety, open communication, listening, and humility."[297]

Detlef Bloecher said that "there is a significant correlation between missionary training and the retention of missionaries on the field."[298] Ruth Wall wrote in International Missionary Training Network the value of "Equipping the Whole Person."[299] Since the 1950s, missionary training has adopted Benjamin Blooms' transformative learning that involves cognitive, affective, and psychomotor, often referred to as the "Head-Heart-Hand" mantra in missions, also known as "know-be-do." This method is currently practiced and seen in bible study group materials, preaching applications, and other training or teaching sessions. Wall challenged this idea by saying that this kind of training focuses on cognitive skills. An essential element neglected in this mantra is the absence of social dimension in learning. Jack Mezirow, in *Transformative Learning*, discusses the interdependency of critical reflection and affective learning. Several authors, Morgan, Coffman, and Sveinunggard, affirm "that critical reflection can only begin once emotions have been validated and worked through."[300]

Though Rational Discourse is an essential medium in transformation, still Merizow attests,

The importance of relationships was found to be the most common finding among all studies reviewed. This contradicts the autonomous and formal nature of transformative learning as we presently understand it, and instead reveals a learning process that is much more dependent on the creation of support, trust, and friendship with others. There is a lack of attention given to the role that relationships play in transformative learning. This omission is demonstrated most directly in the ideal conditions for fostering transformative learning. *It is through building relationships* (emphasis mine) that learners develop the necessary openness and confidence to deal with learning on an affective level, which is essential for managing the threatening and emotionally charged experience of transformation. Without the medium of healthy relationships, critical reflection would seem to be

---

[296] Vella, 85.

[297] Vella , 85-100.

[298] Wan and Hedinger, *Relational Missionary Training*, 189.

[299] Ruth Wall, "Equipping the Whole Person," International Missionary Training Network,last modified February 16, 2015, accessed April 5, 2019, http://www.missionarytraining.org/.

[300] Jack Mezirow and Associates, *Learning as Transformation: Critical Perspectives on a Theory in Progress, 1st ed.* (San Francisco:Jossey-Bass, 2000), 303.

impotent and hollow, lacking the genuine discourse necessary for thoughtful and in-depth reflection.[301]

"Relational knowing of transformative learning refers to the role that relationship with others plays in the transformative process." in other words, effective rational discourse happens when subjective relational elements such as trust, support, humility, friendship are present, crucial for cross-cultural missionaries who need to navigate the intercultural competencies in their new context. For first-generation Filipino missionaries to succeed in the global north, forming good relationships within the team is fundamental. *Training for intercultural missionaries that includes relational building with the new team and the community is essential for transformative learning to happen.*

The world is changing through God's movement of his people across the globe. In this growing need to be relational, "Training based on the Paradigm of Relational Realism is accepted, appreciated, and consistent with lifestyle patterns of most of the non-western world as well as a growing number of Western civilization's younger generations."[302] This relational realism paradigm offers the much-needed missionary mindset shift in this glocal world. The program will use good teaching and outreach methods to serve the relationships, not the opposite.[303]

How do we Define Success in Ministry Using Relational Realism Paradigm

a) Obedience to the Father
   a. " My food is to do the will of Him who sent me and to finish His work" (John 4:34).
b) Perseverance
   a. Matthew 10
c) Relational connections horizontally, whether short term or long term (local church and community)
d) Healthy relationship vertically and horizontally
   a. "Remain in the true Vine who is Jesus Christ and the gardener in the Father. We are the branches; if we remain in the true Vine, we will bear fruit. We bear fruit by loving one another, and we keep His commandments (John 15).
e) Jesus sends an Advocate, the Spirit of Truth from the Father who will testify about him.

The following diagram encapsulates how transformational change occurs when there is a convergence ontologically (horizontal relationships) and pedagogically (teaching methods), primarily manifesting from the individual's relationship with God, divine aid. These vertical relationships include Triune God's activity in the individual lives of the mentors and cross-cultural

---

[301] Jack Mezirow and Associates, 306-08.
[302] Wan and Hedinger, *Relational Missionary Training*, 294.
[303] Wan and Hedinger, *Relational Missionary Training*, 289.

missionaries.[304] Wan emphasized not just "the one on one relationships that fosters transformation, but interaction with the larger group, the Church, the Christian community."[305] In this case, I connected the relationship between the mentors as the *koinonia* and the relationship within the church as their *ecclesia*. In other words, to move the cross-cultural missionary to become interculturally competent and theologically equipped to their new context, God's divine aid and the two horizontal relationships (*koinonia* and *ecclesia*) are essential for transformational change.

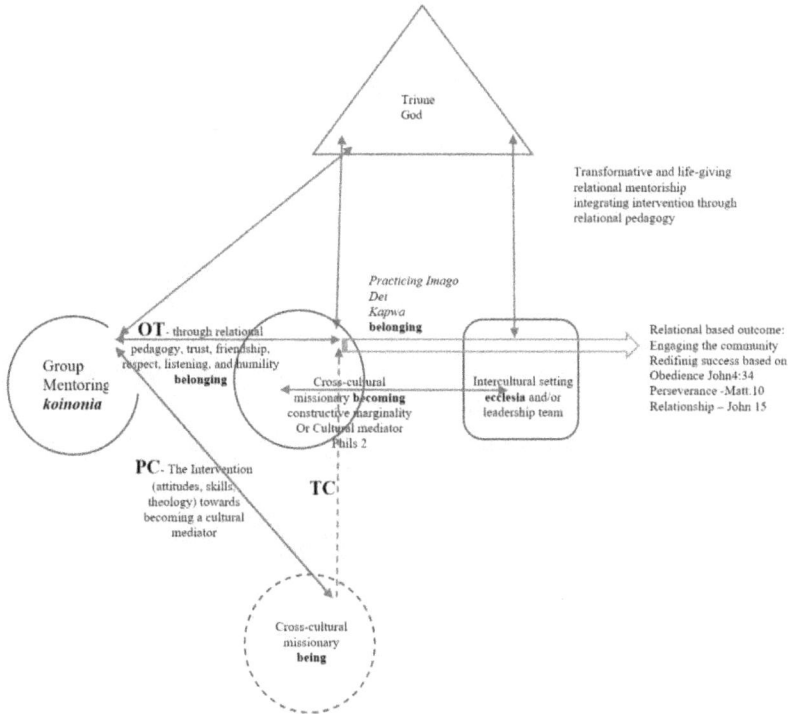

Figure 23 Intervention Through Relational Mentorship and Pedagogy

---

[304] Wan and Hedinger, "Transformative Ministry for the Majority Word Context: Applying Relational Approaches" Occasional Bulletin EMS Spring 2018, PDF.

[305] Wan and Hedinger, "Transformative Ministry for the Majority Word Context: Applying Relational Approaches" Occasional Bulletin EMS Spring 2018, PDF.

BIBLIOGRAPHY

"10 Reasons Why the Global Campus Is the Future of Mission | The Exchange | A Blog by Ed Stetzer." <https://www.christianitytoday.com/edstetzer/2019/july/10-reasons-why-global-campus-is-future-of-mission.html.> (July 29, 2019).Adeney, Miriam. *Kingdom Without Borders: The Untold Story of Global Christianity.* 11/30/09 edition. Downers Grove, Ill: IVP Books, 2009.

Adogame, Afe, Raimundo Barreto, and Wanderley Pereira Da Rosa, eds. *Migration and Public Discourse in World Christianity.* Minneapolis: Fortress Press, 2019.

Alexander Best. "10 Reasons Why the Global Campus Is the Future of Mission." <https://www.christianitytoday.com/edstetzer/2019/july/10-reasons-why-global-campus-is-future-of-mission.html.> (January 1, 2020).

Anderson, Stuart. "National Foundation for American Policy" (n.d.).

Associates, Jack Mezirow and. *Learning as Transformation: Critical Perspectives on a Theory in Progress.* 1 edition. San Francisco: Jossey-Bass, 2000.

"Benevolent Assimilation." *Philippine-American War, 1899-1902.* <https://www.filipinoamericanwar18991902.com/benevolentassimilation.htm.> (May 28, 2021).

"Benevolent Assimilation | Yale University Press." <https://yalebooks.yale.edu/book/9780300030815/benevolent-assimilation.> (May 28, 2021).

"Bill Bright | Cru." *Cru.Org.* <https://www.cru.org/us/en/about/billbright/profile.html.> (January 1, 2020)

Bosch, David J. *Transforming Mission: Paradigm Shifts in Theology of Mission.* 20th Anniversary edition. Maryknoll, N.Y: Orbis, 2011.

Brooks, Rice. *Every Nation In Our Generation: Recovering the Apostolic Mandate.* Lake Mary, Fla. : Brentwood, Tenn: Creation House, 2002.

Chaturvedi, Vinayak. "A Critical Theory of Subalternity: Rethinking Class in Indian Historiography." *Left History: An Interdisciplinary Journal of Historical Inquiry and Debate* 12, no. 1 (November 30, 2007) <https://lh.journals.yorku.ca/index.php/lh/article/view/15042.> (November 25, 2020).

Chinn, Leiton Edward. "Reflections on Reaching the International Student Diaspora in North America." *Global Missiology English* 4, no. 11 (January 7, 2014). <http://ojs.globalmissiology.org/index.php/english/article/view/1684.> (February 26, 2020).

Choi, Bernard C. K., and Anita W. P. Pak. "Multidisciplinarity, Interdisciplinarity and Transdisciplinarity in Health Research, Services, Education and Policy: 1. Definitions, Objectives, and Evidence of Effectiveness." *Clinical and Investigative Medicine. Medecine Clinique Et Experimentale* 29, no. 6 (December 2006): 351–364.

"Country: Philippines." *Lausanne Movement.* Last modified December 17, 2012. <https://www.lausanne.org/tbd/country-profiles/philippines.> (October 22, 2020)

Cypress, Brigitte S. "Rigor or Reliability and Validity in Qualitative Research: Perspectives, Strategies, Reconceptualization, and Recommendations." *Dimensions of Critical Care Nursing* 36, no. 4 (August 2017): 253–263. <https://journals.lww.com/dccnjournal/Fulltext/2017/07000/Rigor_or_Reliability_and_Validity_in_Qualitative.6.aspx.>)January 18, 2021.

"Diaspora Missiology: Part 1 – Missiologically Thinking." <https://www.jdpayne.org/2010/04/diaspora-missiology-part-1/.> (September 2020).

"Equipping the Whole Person." Last modified February 16, 2015. <http://www.missionarytraining.org/mt/index.php/forum/bulletin-no-1-equipping-the-whole-person/3-equipping-the-whole-person.> (April 5, 2010).

Escosar, Dr Jun, and Walter Walker. *A Bible and a Passport: Obeying the Call to Make Disciples in Every Nation.* Every Nation Productions, 2019.

"Filipino Immigrants." *Immigration to the United States.* <https://immigrationtounitedstates.org/497-filipino-immigrants.html.> (March 9, 2020).

Gallagher, Robert L. *Encountering the History of Missions.* Grand Rapids, Michigan: Baker Academic, 2017.

George, Sam. *Diaspora Christianities: Global Scattering and Gathering of South Asian Christians.* Fortress Press, 2019.

Gilbert. *Missiological Research: Interdisciplinary Foundations, Methods, and Integration.* Edited by Marvin Gilbert, Alan R. Johnson, and Paul W. Lewis. William Carey Library Publishing, 2018.

glpadmin. "Dr. Jane Vella." *Global Learning Partners*. Last modified February 6, 2018. <https://www.globallearningpartners.com/the-team/jane-vella/.> (May 7, 201).

Goodacre, Mark, *The Case Against Q: Studies in Markan Priority and the Synoptic Problem* (Harrisburg, PA: Trinity Press International, 2002).

Gorospe, Athena E. "Case Study: Overseas Filipino Workers (LOP 62 G)." *Lausanne Movement*. Last modified February 1, 2007. <https://www.lausanne.org/content/lop/case-study-overseas-filipino-workers-lop-62-g.> (January 1, 2020).

Grady, J. Lee. "Why Relational Discipleship Has Become My Priority." *Charisma News*. <https://www.charismanews.com/opinion/33499-why-relational-discipleship-has-become-my-priority.> (February 2, 2021).

Hiebert, Paul G. *The Gospel in Human Contexts: Anthropological Explorations for Contemporary Missions*. Illustrated edition. Grand Rapids, Michigan: Baker Academic, 2009.

Hoffman, Dr Edwin, and Arjan Verdooren. *Diversity Competence: Cultures Don't Meet, People Do*. CABI, 2019.

Holloway, Immy, and Lorraine Brown. *Essentials of a Qualitative Doctorate*. 1st edition. Walnut Creek, Calif: Routledge, 2012.

Hunt, Keith, and Gladys Hunt. *For Christ and the University: The Story of InterVarsity Christian Fellowship of the USA - 1940-1990*. Downers Grove, Ill: IVP Books, 1992.

"InterVarsity." *InterVarsity*. <https://intervarsity.org/.> (January 1, 2020).

Jenkins, Philip. *The Next Christendom: The Coming of Global Christianity*. 3 edition. Oxford ; New York: Oxford University Press, 2011.

Jocano, Felipe Landa Jacano, *Filipino World: Ethnographic of Local Knowledge*. Metro Manila, Philippines, 1998.

Johnson, Robert Burke, and Larry B. Christensen. *Educational Research: Quantitative, Qualitative, and Mixed Approaches*. 6th Edition. SAGE Publications, Inc, 2016.

"Jonathan Morrow on Building Lasting Faith in Gen Z." *Barna Group*. Last modified July 19, 2018. <https://www.barna.com/gen-z-qa-with-jonathan-morrow/.> (May 13, 2021).

"Kapwa | Kapwa Is Self in Other, Pakikipagkapwa Is Sacred Interconnection," n.d. <http://pakikipagkapwa.org/.> (November 24, 2020).

Kurtulmus, Mehmet. "The Effect of Diversity Climate Perception on Alienation of Students to University." *International Journal of Higher Education* 5, no. 1

(2016): 141–151. <https://eric.ed.gov/?id=EJ1088676.> (November 5, 2020).

Lincoln, Yvonna S., and Egon G. Guba. *Naturalistic Inquiry*. SAGE, 1985.

Loritts, Bryan. *Right Color, Wrong Culture: The Type of Leader Your Organization Needs to Become Multiethnic*. New Edition. Chicago: Moody Publishers, 2014.

Ma, Jaeson, and Lou Engle. *The Blueprint: A Revolutionary Plan to Plant Missional Communities on Campus*. Chosen Books, 2007.

McDowell, Sean. *So the Next Generation Will Know*. Colorado Springs, CO: David C Cook - TBG, 2019.

McGavran, Donald A. *Understanding Church Growth*. Wm. B. Eerdmans Publishing, 1990.

Meyer, Erin. The Culture Map. New York, NY: Public Affairs, 2015.

Moreau, A. Scott. *Contextualization in World Missions: Mapping and Assessing Evangelical Models*. Grand Rapids, MI: Kregel Publications, 2012.

Murrell, Steve. *100 Years From Now: Sustaining a Movement for Generations*. 1st Edition. Dunham Books, 2013.

____ *WikiChurch: Making Discipleship Engaging, Empowering, and Viral*. Illustrated edition. Lake Mary, Fla: Charisma House, 2011.

Noll, Mark A. *The New Shape of World Christianity: How American Experience Reflects Global Faith*. IVP Academic, 2009.

Norton, H. Wilbert, Sr. "The Student Foreign Missions Fellowship over Fifty-Five Years." *International Bulletin of Missionary Research* 17, no. 1 (January 1993): 17-.

"Optimism vs. Pessimism • Kapwa Theory (Virgilio G. Enriquez) In Filipino,..." *Optimism vs. Pessimism*. <https://ani-eusebio.> (February 15, 2021).

"Philippines Population 2020 (Demographics, Maps, Graphs)." <http://worldpopulationreview.com/countries/philippines-population/.> (February 27, 2020).

Plueddemann, James E. *Leading Across Cultures: Effective Ministry and Mission in the Global Church*. 5899th edition. Downers Grove, Ill: IVP Academic, 2009.

Pocock, Michael, and Enoch Wan, eds. *Diaspora Missiology: Reflections on Reaching the Scattered Peoples of the World*. William Carey Library, 2015.

Rayudu, C.S. *Communication*. Mumbai, India: Global Media, 2009. Accessed March 2, 2021. http://ebookcentral.proquest.com/lib/westernseminary-ebooks/detail.action?docID=3011271.

Robert, Bob Jr., *Glocalization: How Followers of Jesus Engage a Flat World*, Grand Rapids,MI: Zondervan, 2007.

Reese, Randy D., Robert Loane, and Eugene Peterson. *Deep Mentoring: Guiding Others on Their Leadership Journey.* IVP Books, 2012.

San Juan, E, *From Exile to Diaspora: Versions of the Filipino Experience in the United States,* Boulder, CO, Westview Press, 1998.

Scattered and Gathered: A Global Compendium of Diaspora Missiology. Oxford, England: Regnum Books International, 2016.

"Seattle, United States Population (2021) - Population Stat," <https://populationstat.com/united-states/seattle.> (October 27, 2021).

"Seattle - OPCD | Seattle.Gov," <http://www.seattle.gov/opcd/population-and-demographics/about-seattle#raceethnicity.> (October 27, 2021).

Smith, Donald K. *Creating Understanding: Christian Communication Across Cultural Landscapes.* 1 edition. Books On Creating Understanding, 2014.

"Social Media, Social Life Infographic | Common Sense Media." <https://www.commonsensemedia.org/social-media-social-life-infographic.> (July 26, 2019).

"Table 2 : Top Ten Host Countries for International Students: Global..." *ResearchGate.* <https://www.researchgate.net/figure/Top-ten-host-countries-for-international-students-global-total-and-UK-origin-students_tbl2_257305635.> (February 24, 2020).

"The Number of International Migrants Reaches 272 Million, Continuing an Upward Trend in All World Regions, Says UN." *UN DESA | United Nations Department of Economic and Social Affairs.* Last modified September 17, 2019. <https://www.un.org/development/desa/en/news/population/international-migrant-stock-2019.html.. (February 26, 2020).

Thurmond, Veronica A. "The Point of Triangulation." *Journal of Nursing Scholarship* 33, no. 3 (September 2001): 253–258. <http://doi.wiley.com/10.1111/j.1547-5069.2001.00253.x.> (November 30, 2020).

Tira, Sadiri Joy, and Stuart Lightbody. *1 a Cyclical, Glocal Diaspora Congregation: A Case Study of the First Filipino Alliance Church*, 1984.

Triandis, Harry C., and H C Triandis. "Individualism-Collectivism and Personality." *Journal of Personality* 69, no. 6 (December 2001): 907–924. <http://search.ebscohost.com> (April 29, 2021).

Turner, John G. *Bill Bright and Campus Crusade for Christ: The Renewal of Evangelicalism in Postwar America*. First Edition. Chapel Hill: The University of North Carolina Press, 2008.

Vella, Jane. Learning to Listen Learning to Teach: The Power of Dialogue in Educating Adults. San Francisco, CA: Joseey-Bass, 2002.

Viernes, Sr. Ramona M. O.P. and Allan B. de Guzman, "Filipino Teachers' Experiences of Supportive Relationships with Colleagues: A Narrative-biographical Inquiry," Asia Pacific Education Review2005, Vol. 6, No. 2, 137-142. Education Research Institute.

Volf, Miroslav. *Exclusion and Embrace, Revised and Updated: A Theological Exploration of Identity, Otherness, and Reconciliation*. Revised, Updated edition. Nashville, TN: Abingdon Press, 2019.

Wan, Enoch. *Diaspora Missiology: Theory, Methodology, and Practice*, Portland, OR: Institute of Diaspora Studies-USA, 2011.

Wan, Enoch, Dennis C. Bradford, Leiton E. Chinn, Lisa Espineli Chinn, Sam Green, William Murrel, Katie J. Rawsom, Christopher D. Sneller, Florence PL Tan, and Chin T. Wang. *Diaspora Missions to International Students*. Western Seminary Press, 2019.

Wan, Enoch, and Anthony Casey. *Church Planting among Immigrants in US Urban Centers (Second Edition): The "Where", "Why", And "How" of Diaspora*. 2 edition. Portland, OR: CreateSpace Independent Publishing Platform, 2016.

Wan, Enoch, and Mark Hedinger. *Relational Missionary Training: Theology, Theory & Practice*. Skyforest, CA: Urban Loft Publishers, 2017.

Wan, Enoch, and Mark Hedinger, "Transformative Ministry for the Majority Word Context: Applying Relational Approaches" Occasional Bulletin EMS Spring 2018, PDF.

Wan, Enoch and Shane Mikeska. Engaging the Secular World Through Life-on-Life Discipleship in the British Context: Relational Paradigm in Action. Portland, OR:Western Seminary Press, 2020.

Wan, Enoch, and Sadiri Joy Tira. "The Filipino Experience in Diaspora Missions: A Case Study Of Mission Initiatives From The Majority World Churches" PDF.

Wan, Enoch, "Relational Transformational Leadership: An Asian Perspective," "Asian Mission Advance" April 2021, PDF

Warner, +J. "Are Young People Really Leaving Christianity?" *Cold Case Christianity*, January 12, 2019. <https://coldcasechristianity.com/writings/are-young-people-really-leaving-christianity/.> (July 26, 2019).

"What Is The Global South?" *WorldAtlas.*
<https://www.worldatlas.com/articles/what-is-the-global-south.html.>
(October 8, 2020).

"What Makes Filipino, Filipino?" A presentation by Felipe De Leon Jr.

<https://athenspe.dfa.gov.ph/newsroom/community-news> (Novmeber 4,
2021).

"What's the Significance of Simon Carrying Jesus's Cross?" *Desiring God.* Last
modified April 19, 2019. <https://www.desiringgod.org/interviews/whats-
the-significance-of-simon-carrying-jesuss-cross.> (April 8, 2020).

"World Leaders Study in the United States." *Study in the States.* Last modified
November 8, 2012. <https://studyinthestates.dhs.gov> (March 12, 2020)

Wright, Christopher J. H. *The Mission of God: Unlocking the Bible's Grand
Narrative.* Edition Unstated. Downers Grove, Ill: IVP Academic, 2006.

Wright, Christopher J.H. The Mission of God's People: A Biblical Theology of the
Church's Mission. Grand Rapids, MI:Zondervan, 2010.

Yeh, Allen. *Polycentric Missiology: 21st-Century Mission from Everyone to
Everywhere.* Downers Grove: IVP Academic, 2016.

Zachary, Lois J. *The Mentor's Guide: Facilitating Effective Learning Relationships.*
2 edition. San Francisco: Jossey-Bass, 2011.

Zaide, Sonia M. *The Philippines: A Unique Nation.* All-Nations Publishing, 1999.

Zhou, Youyou. "The Impact of Chinese Students in the US, Charted and Mapped."
Quartz. <https://qz.com/1410768/the-number-of-chinese-students-in-the-
us-charted-and-mapped/.> (March 6, 2019)

www.ingramcontent.com/pod-product-compliance
Lightning Source LLC
Chambersburg PA
CBHW061824040426
42447CB00012B/2812